12th Meeting of the Special Interest Group on Computational Morphology and Phonology 2012

(SIGMORPHON 2012)

AA004624

Held at the 2012 Conference of the North American Chapter of the Association for Computational Linguistics: Human Language Technologies (NAACL-HLT 2012)

Montreal, Quebec, Canada
3-8 June 2012

ISBN: 978-1-62276-551-5

Printed from e-media with permission by:

Curran Associates, Inc.
57 Morehouse Lane
Red Hook, NY 12571

Some format issues inherent in the e-media version may also appear in this print version.

Copyright© (2012) by the Association for Computational Linguistics
All rights reserved.

Printed by Curran Associates, Inc. (2013)

For permission requests, please contact the Association for Computational Linguistics at the address below.

Association for Computational Linguistics
209 N. Eighth Street
Stroudsburg, Pennsylvania 18360

Phone: 1-570-476-8006
Fax: 1-570-476-0860

acl@aclweb.org

Additional copies of this publication are available from:

Curran Associates, Inc.
57 Morehouse Lane
Red Hook, NY 12571 USA
Phone: 845-758-0400
Fax: 845-758-2634
Email: curran@proceedings.com
Web: www.proceedings.com

Introduction

We are delighted to present the Proceedings of the Twelfth Meeting of the ACL Special Interest Group on Computational Morphology and Phonology (SIGMORPHON), to be held on June 7, 2012 at Le Centre Sheraton Montréal, Montréal, Canada. The purpose of SIGMORPHON is to foster computational research on the phonological, morphological, and phonetic properties of human language. All three of these sub-areas deal largely with the local structure of words and so share many technical methods. Furthermore, computational work that models empirical data must often draw on at least two of these areas, with explicit consideration of the morphology-phonology or phonology-phonetics interface. In recent years the remit has expanded to also include research on orthographic issues such as transliteration and variable spelling.

We received a good number of submissions, on the full range of sub-areas, and accepted around sixty percent. This has enabled us to provide what we hope you will agree is a high quality program.

We are grateful to the program committee for their careful and thoughtful reviews and discussions of the papers submitted this year. We hope that you enjoy the workshop and these proceedings.

Lynne Cahill
Adam Albright

Organizers:

Lynne Cahill, Univeristy of Brighton (UK)
Adam Albright, MIT (USA)

Program Committee:

Jason Eisner, Johns Hopkins University (USA)
Mark Ellison, University of Western Australia (Australia)
Roger Evans, University of Brighton (UK)
Sharon Goldwater, University of Edinburgh (UK)
Jeffrey Heinz, University of Delaware (USA)
Jon Herring, British Library (UK)
William Idsardi, University of Maryland (USA)
Gaja Jarosz, Yale University (USA)
Greg Kobele, University of Chicago (USA)
Grzegorz Kondrak, University of Alberta (Canada)
Kimmo Koskenniemi, University of Helsinki (Finland)
Mikko Kurimo, TKK (Finland)
Karen Livescu, Toyota Technological Institute at University of Chicago (USA)
Giorgio Magri, IJN, ENS (France)
Katya Pertsova, University of North Carolina (USA)
Jason Riggle, University of Chicago (USA)
Shuly Wintner, University of Haifa (Israel)

Table of Contents

Conference Program

Thursday June 7, 2012

9:00	Welcome
9:15–9:45	*A Morphological Analyzer for Egyptian Arabic* Nizar Habash, Ramy Eskander and Abdelati Hawwari
9:45–10:15	*Hindi Derivational Morphological Analyzer* Nikhil Kanuparthi, Abhilash Inumella and Dipti Misra Sharma
10:15-10:30	Discussion
10:30-11:00	Coffee break
11:00–11:30	*Phrase-Based Approach for Adaptive Tokenization* Jianqiang Ma and Dale Gerdemann
11:30–12:00	*A Regularized Compression Method to Unsupervised Word Segmentation* Ruey-Cheng Chen, Chiung-Min Tsai and Jieh Hsiang
12:00–12:30	*A rule-based approach to unknown word recognition in Arabic* Lynne Cahill
12:30-12:45	Discussion
12:45-2:00	Lunch
2:00–2:30	*Bounded copying is subsequential: Implications for metathesis and reduplication* Jane Chandlee and Jeffrey Heinz
2:30–3:00	*An approximation approach to the problem of the acquisition of phonotactics in Optimality Theory* Giorgio Magri
3:00–3:30	*Learning probabilities over underlying representations* Joe Pater, Robert Staubs, Karen Jesney and Brian Smith

Thursday June 7, 2012 (continued)

3:30-4:00	Coffee break
4:00–4:30	*Linguistic categorization and complexity* Katya Pertsova
4:30-4:45	Discussion
4:45-5:15	Business meeting (all are welcome to attend)

A Morphological Analyzer for Egyptian Arabic

Nizar Habash and **Ramy Eskander** and **Abdelati Hawwari**
Center for Computational Learning Systems
Columbia University
New York, NY, USA
{habash,reskander,ahawwari}@ccls.columbia.edu

Abstract

Most tools and resources developed for natural language processing of Arabic are designed for Modern Standard Arabic (MSA) and perform terribly on Arabic dialects, such as Egyptian Arabic. Egyptian Arabic differs from MSA phonologically, morphologically and lexically and has no standardized orthography. We present a linguistically accurate, large-scale morphological analyzer for Egyptian Arabic. The analyzer extends an existing resource, the Egyptian Colloquial Arabic Lexicon, and follows the part-of-speech guidelines used by the Linguistic Data Consortium for Egyptian Arabic. It accepts multiple orthographic variants and normalizes them to a conventional orthography.

1 Introduction

Dialectal Arabic (DA) refers to the day-to-day native vernaculars spoken in the Arab World. DA is used side by side with Modern Standard Arabic (MSA), the official language of the media and education (Holes, 2004). Although DAs are historically related to MSA, there are many phonological, morphological and lexical differences between them. Unlike MSA, DAs have no standard orthographies or language academies. Furthermore, different DAs, such as Egyptian Arabic (henceforth, EGY), Levantine Arabic or Moroccan Arabic have important differences among them similar to those seen among Romance languages (Erwin, 1963; Cowell, 1964; Abdel-Massih et al., 1979; Holes, 2004). Most tools and resources developed for natural language processing (NLP) of Arabic are designed for MSA. Such resources are quite limited when it comes to processing DA, e.g., a state-of-the-art MSA morphological analyzer has been reported to only have 60% coverage of Levantine Arabic verb forms (Habash and Rambow, 2006). Most efforts to address this gap have been lacking. Some have taken a quick-and-dirty approach to model shallow morphology in DA by extending MSA tools, resulting in linguistically inaccurate models (Abo Bakr et al., 2008; Salloum and Habash, 2011). Others have attempted to build linguistically accurate models that are lacking in coverage (at the lexical or inflectional levels) or focusing on representations that are not readily usable for NLP text processing, e.g., phonological lexicons (Kilany et al., 2002).

In this paper we present the Columbia Arabic Language and dIalect Morphological Analyzer (CALIMA) for EGY.[1] We built this tool by extending an existing resource for EGY, the Egyptian Colloquial Arabic Lexicon (ECAL) (Kilany et al., 2002). CALIMA is a linguistically accurate, large-scale morphological analyzer. It follows the part-of-speech (POS) guidelines used by the Linguistic Data Consortium for EGY (Maamouri et al., 2012b). It accepts multiple orthographic variants and normalizes them to CODA, a conventional orthography for DA (Habash et al., 2012).

The rest of the paper is structured as follows: Section 2 presents relevant motivating linguistic facts. Section 3 discusses related work. Section 4 details the steps taken to create CALIMA starting with ECAL. Section 5 presents a preliminary evaluation and statistics about the coverage of CALIMA. Finally, Section 6 outlines future plans and directions.

[1] Although we focus on Egyptian Arabic in this paper, the CALIMA name will be used in the future to cover a variety of dialects.

2 Motivating Linguistic Facts

We present some general Arabic (MSA/DA) NLP challenges. Then we discuss differences between MSA and DA – specifically EGY.

2.1 General Arabic Linguistic Challenges

Arabic, as MSA or DA, poses many challenges for NLP. Arabic is a morphologically complex language which includes rich inflectional morphology, expressed both templatically and affixationally, and several classes of attachable clitics. For example, the MSA word وسيكتبونها *wa+sa+ya-ktub-uwna+hA*[2] 'and they will write it' has two proclitics (+و *wa+* 'and' and +س *sa+* 'will'), one prefix -ي *ya-* '3rd person', one suffix ون- *-uwna* 'masculine plural' and one pronominal enclitic ها+ *+hA* 'it/her'. The stem *ktub* can be further analyzed into the root *ktb* and pattern *12u3*.

Additionally, Arabic is written with optional diacritics that primarily specify short vowels and consonantal doubling, e.g., the example above will most certainly be written as *wsyktbwnhA*. The absence of these diacritics together with the language's complex morphology lead to a high degree of ambiguity, e.g., the Standard Arabic Morphological Analyzer (SAMA) (Graff et al., 2009) produces an average of 12 analyses per MSA word.

Moreover, some letters in Arabic are often spelled inconsistently which leads to an increase in both sparsity (multiple forms of the same word) and ambiguity (same form corresponding to multiple words), e.g., variants of the Hamzated Alif, أ Â or إ Ǎ, are often written without their Hamza (ء '): ا *A*. and the Alif-Maqsura (or dot-less Ya) ى ý and the regular dotted Ya ي *y* are often used interchangeably in the word-final position (Buckwalter, 2007).

Arabic complex morphology and ambiguity are handled using tools for disambiguation and tokenization (Habash and Rambow, 2005; Diab et al., 2007).

[2]Arabic orthographic transliteration is presented in the HSB scheme (Habash et al., 2007): (in alphabetical order)
ا ب ت ث ج ح خ د ذ ر ز س ش ص ض ط ظ ع غ ف ق ك ل م ن ه و ي
A b t θ j H x d ð r z s š S D T Ď ς γ f q k l m n h w y
and the additional letters: ' ء, Â أ, Ǎ إ, Ā آ, ŵ ؤ, ŷ ئ, ħ ة, ý ى.

We distinguish between *morphological analysis*, whose target is to produce all possible morphological/POS readings of a word out of context, and *morphological disambiguation*, which attempts to tag the word in context (Habash and Rambow, 2005). The work presented in this paper is only about *morphological analysis*.

2.2 Differences between MSA and DA

Contemporary Arabic is in fact a collection of varieties: MSA, which has a standard orthography and is used in formal settings, and DAs, which are commonly used informally and with increasing presence on the web, but which do not have standard orthographies. DAs mostly differ from MSA phonologically, morphologically, and lexically (Gadalla, 2000; Holes, 2004). These difference are not modeled as part of MSA NLP tools, leaving a gap in coverage when using them to process DAs. All examples below are in Egyptian Arabic (EGY).

Phonologically, the profile of EGY is quite similar to MSA, except for some important differences. For example, the MSA consonants ق/ذ/ث *q/ð/θ* are generally pronounced in EGY (Cairene) as *'/z/s* (Holes, 2004). Some of these consonants shift in different ways in different words: e.g., MSA ذنب *ðanb* 'fault' and كذب *kiðb* 'lying' are pronounced *zanb* and *kidb*. EGY has five long vowels compared with MSA's three long vowels. Unlike MSA, long vowels in EGY predictably shorten under certain conditions, often as a result of cliticization. For example, compare the following forms of the same verb: شاف *šAf* /šāf/ 'he saw' and شافها *šAf+hA* /šafha/ 'he saw her' (Habash et al., 2012).

Morphologically, the most important difference is in the use of clitics and affixes that do not exist in MSA. For instance, the EGY equivalent of the MSA example above is وحيكتبوها *wi+Ha+yi-ktib-uw+hA* 'and they will write it'. The optionality of vocalic diacritics helps hide some of the differences resulting from vowel changes; compare the undiacritized forms: EGY *wHyktbwhA* and MSA *wsyktbwnhA*. In this example, the forms of the clitics and affixes are different in EGY although they have the same meaning; however, EGY has clitics that are not part of MSA morphology, e.g., the indirect pronominal object clitic (*+l+uh* 'for him')

وحيكتبوهاله *wi+Ha+yi-ktib-uw+hA+l+uh* 'and they will write it for him'. Another important example is the circumfix negation +ما+ +ش *mA+* +š which surrounds some verb forms: ماكتبش *mA+katab+š* 'he did not write' (the MSA equivalent is two words: لم يكتب *lam yaktub*). Another important morphological difference from MSA is that DAs in general and not just EGY drop the case and mood features almost completely.

Lexically, the number of differences is very large. Examples include بس *bas* 'only', طربيزة *tarabayzah̄* 'table', مرات *mirAt* 'wife [of]' and دول *dawl* 'these', which correspond to MSA فقط *faqaT*, طاولة *TAwilah̄*, زوجة *zawjah̄* and هؤلاء *haŵlA'*, respectively.

An important challenge for NLP work on DAs in general is the lack of an orthographic standard. EGY writers are often inconsistent even in their own writing. The differences in phonology between MSA and EGY are often responsible: words can be spelled as pronounced or etymologically in their related MSA form, e.g., كدب *kidb* or كذب *kiðb*. Some clitics have multiple common forms, e.g., the future particle ح *Ha* appears as a separate word or as a proclitic +ح/+ه *Ha+/ha+*, reflecting different pronunciations. The different spellings may add some confusion, e.g., كتبو *ktbw* may be كتبوا *katabuwA* 'they wrote' or كتبه *katabuh* 'he wrote it'. Finally, shortened long vowels can be spelled long or short, e.g., شافها/شفها *šAf+hA/šf+hA* 'he saw her'.

3 Related Work

3.1 Approaches to Arabic Morphology

There has been a considerable amount of work on Arabic morphological analysis (Al-Sughaiyer and Al-Kharashi, 2004; Habash, 2010). Altantawy et al. (2011) characterize the various approaches explored for Arabic and Semitic computational morphology as being on a continuum with two poles: on one end, very abstract and linguistically rich representations and morphological rules are used to derive surface forms; while on the other end, simple and shallow techniques focus on efficient search in a space of precompiled (tabulated) solutions. The first type is typically implemented using finite-state technology and can be at many different degrees of sophistication and detail (Beesley et al., 1989; Kiraz, 2000; Habash and Rambow, 2006). The second type is typically implemented using hash-tables with a simple search algorithm. Examples include the Buckwalter Arabic Morphological Analyzer (BAMA) (Buckwalter, 2004), its Standard Arabic Morphological Analyzer (SAMA) (Graff et al., 2009) incarnation, and their generation-oriented extension, ALMOR (Habash, 2007). These systems do not represent the morphemic, phonological and orthographic rules directly, and instead compile their effect into the lexicon itself, which consists of three tables for prefixes, stems and suffixes and their compatibilities. A prefix or suffix in this approach is a string consisting of all the word's prefixes and suffixes, respectively, as a single unit (including null affix sequences). During analysis, all possible splits of a word into compatible prefix-stem-suffix combination are explored. More details are discussed in Section 4.5. Numerous intermediate points exist between these two extremes (e.g., ElixirFM (Smrž, 2007)). Altantawy et al. (2011) describe a method for converting a linguistically complex and abstract implementation of Arabic verbs in finite-state machinery into a simple precompiled tabular representation.

The approach we follow in this paper is closer to the second type. We start with a lexicon of inflected forms and derive from it a tabular representation compatible with the SAMA system for MSA. However, as we do this, we design the tables and extend them in ways that capture generalizations and extend orthographic coverage.

3.2 Arabic Dialect Morphology

The majority of the work discussed above has focused on MSA, while only a few efforts have targeted DA morphology (Kilany et al., 2002; Riesa and Yarowsky, 2006; Habash and Rambow, 2006; Abo Bakr et al., 2008; Salloum and Habash, 2011; Mohamed et al., 2012). These efforts generally fall in two camps. First are solutions that focus on extending MSA tools to cover DA phenomena. For example, both Abo Bakr et al. (2008) and Salloum and Habash (2011) extended the BAMA/SAMA databases (Buckwalter, 2004; Graff et al., 2009) to accept DA prefixes and suffixes. Both of these efforts were interested in mapping DA text to some MSA-like form; as such they did not model DA linguistic phenomena, e.g., the ADAM system (Salloum and Habash, 2011) outputs only MSA diacritics that are discarded in later processing.

The second camp is interested in modeling DA directly. However, the attempts at doing so are lacking in coverage in one dimension or another. The earliest effort on EGY that we know of is the Egyptian Colloquial Arabic Lexicon (ECAL) (Kilany et al., 2002). It was developed as part of the CALLHOME Egyptian Arabic (CHE) corpus (Gadalla et al., 1997) which contains 140 telephone conversations and their transcripts. The lexicon lists all of the words appearing in the CHE corpus and provides phonological, orthographic and morphological information for them. This is an important resource; however, it is lacking in many ways: the orthographic forms are undiacritized, no morpheme segmentations are provided, and the lexicon has only some 66K fully inflected forms and as such lacks general morphological coverage. Another effort is the work by Habash and Rambow (2006) which focuses on modeling DAs together with MSA using a common multi-tier finite-state-machine framework. Although this approach has a lot of potential, in practice, it is closer to the first camp in its results since they used MSA lexicons as a base. Finally, two previous efforts focused on modeling shallow dialectal segmentation using supervised methods (Riesa and Yarowsky, 2006; Mohamed et al., 2012). Riesa and Yarowsky (2006) presented a supervised algorithm for online morpheme segmentation for Iraqi Arabic that cut the out-of-vocabulary rates by half in the context of machine translation into English. Mohamed et al. (2012) annotated a collection of EGY for morpheme boundaries and used this data to develop an EGY tokenizer. Although these efforts model DA directly, they remain at a shallow level of representation (undiacritized surface morph segmentation).

We use the ECAL lexicon as a base for CALIMA and extend it further. Some of the expansion techniques we used are inspired by previous solutions (Abo Bakr et al., 2008; Salloum and Habash, 2011). For the morphological representation, we follow the Linguistic Data Consortium guidelines which extend the MSA POS guidelines to multiple dialects (Maamouri et al., 2006; Maamouri et al., 2012b). To address the problem of orthographic variations, we follow the proposal by Habash et al. (2012) who designed a conventional orthography for DA (or CODA) for NLP applications in the CALIMA databases. However, to handle input in a variety of spellings, we extend our analyzer to accept non-CODA-compliant word forms but map them only to CODA-compliant forms as part of the analysis.

4 Approach

We describe next the various steps for creating CALIMA starting with ECAL. The details of the approach are to some degree dependent on this unique resource; however, some aspects of the approach may be generalizable to other resources, and languages or dialects.

4.1 The Egyptian Colloquial Arabic Lexicon

ECAL has about 66K entries: 27K verbs, 36K nouns and adjectives, 1.5K proper nouns and 1K closed classes. For each entry, the lexicon provides a phonological form, an undiacritized Arabic script orthography, a lemma (in phonological form), and morphological features, among other information. There are 36K unique lemmas and 1,464 unique morphological feature combinations. The following is an example ECAL entry for the word مبيكلموش *mbyklmwš* 'he did not talk to him'.[3] We only show Arabic orthography, phonology, and lemma+features:

```
mbyklmwš
mabiykallimU$⁴
kallim:verb+pres-3rd-masc-sg+DO-3rd-masc-sg+neg
```

Our goal for CALIMA is to have a much larger coverage, a CODA-compliant diacritized orthography, and a morpheme-based morphological analysis. The next steps allow us to accomplish these goals.

4.2 Diacritic Insertion

First, we built a component to diacritize the ECAL undiacritized Arabic script entries in a way that is consistent with ECAL phonological form. This was implemented using a finite-state transducer (FST) that maps the phonological form to multiple possible

[3]The same orthographic form has another reading 'they did not talk' which of course has different morphological features.

[4]The phonological form as used in ECAL. For transcription details, see (Kilany et al., 2002).

diacritized Arabic script forms. The form that is the same as the undiacritized ECAL orthography (except for diacritics) is used as the diacritized orthography for the rest of the process. The FST consists of about 160 transformations that we created manually. All except for 100 cases are generic mappings, e.g., two repeated *b* consonants are turned into بّ *b∼*,[5] or a short vowel *u* can be orthographically a short vowel (just the diacritic *u*) or a long vowel *uw* which shortened. The exceptional 100 cases were specified by hand in the FST as complete string mappings. These were mostly odd spellings of foreign words or spelling errors. We did not attempt to correct or change the ECAL letter spelling; we only added diacritics.

After diacritization, we modify the Arabic orthography in the example above to: `mabiykal~imuwš`.

4.3 Morphological Tag Mapping

Next, we wrote rules to convert from ECAL diacritized Arabic and morphology to CODA-compliant diacritized Arabic and LDC EGY POS compliant tags. The rules fall into three categories: ignore rules specify which ECAL entries to exclude due to errors; correction rules correct for some ECAL entry errors; and prefix/suffix/stem rules are used to identify specific pairs of prefix/suffix/stem substrings and morphological features to map to appropriate prefix/suffix/stem morphemes, respectively. For stems, the majority of the rules also identify roots and patterns. Since multiple root-pattern combinations may be possible for a particular word, the appropriate root-pattern is chosen by enforcing consistency across all the inflected forms of the lemma of the word and minimizing the overall number of roots in the system. We do not use or report on root-patterns in CALIMA in this paper since this information is not required by the LDC tags; however, we plan on using them in future efforts exploiting templatic morphology.

At the time of writing this paper, the system included 4,632 rules covering all POS. These include 1,248 ignore rules, 1,451 correction rules, 83 prefix rules, and 441 suffixes rules. About 1,409 stem rules are used to map core POS tags and identify templatic roots and patterns. Some rules were semi-automatically created, but all were manually checked. The rules are specified in a simple format that is interpreted and applied by a separate rule processing script. Developing the script and writing the rules took about 3 person-months of effort.

As an example, the following three rules are used to handle the circumfix *ma++š* 'not' and the progressing particle *bi+*.

```
PRE: ma,+neg   =>  ϕ,+neg   >> mA/NEG_PART#
PRE: bi,+pres  =>  ϕ,+subj  >> bi/PROG_PART+
SUF: š,+neg    =>   ϕ,ϕ      >> +š/NEG_PART
```

The input to the rule processor is a pair of surface form and morphological features. Each rule matches on a surface substring and a combination of morphological features (first two comma-separated tokens in the rule) and rewrites the parts it matched on (second two comma-separated tokens in the rule after =>). The type of the rule, i.e. prefix or suffix rule, determines how the matching is applied. In addition, the rule generates a substring of the target tag (last token in the rule). The first and third rules above handle a circumfix; the *+neg* feature is not deleted in the first rule (which handles the prefix) to allow the third rule (which handles the suffix) to fire. The second rule rewrites the feature *+pres* (present tense) as *+subj* (subjunctive) which is consistent with the form of the verb after removing the progressive particle *bi+*. After applying these rules in addition to a few others, the above example is turned into CODA and EGY POS compliant forms (# means word boundary):[6]

```
mA#bi+yi+kal~im+huw+š
NEG_PART#PROG_PART+IV3MS+IV+IVSUFF_DO:3MS+NEG_PART
```

The stem rules, whose results are not shown here, determine that the root is *klm* and the pattern is *1a22i3*.

We extended the set of mapped ECAL entries systematically. We copied entries and modified them to include additional clitics that are not present with all entries, e.g., the conjunction +ف *fa+* 'then', and the definite article +ال *Al+*.

4.4 Orthographic Lemma Identification

The ECAL lemmas are specified in a phonological form, e.g., in the example above, it is *kallim*. To determine the diacritized Arabic orthography spelling

[5]The ∼ diacritic or *Shadda* indicates the presence of consonantal doubling.

[6]CODA guidelines state that the negative particle ما *mA* is not to be cliticized except in a very small number of words (Habash et al., 2012).

of the lemma, we relied on the existence of the lemma itself as an entry and other ad hoc rules to identify the appropriate form. Using this technique, we successfully identified the orthographic lemma form for 97% of the cases. The remainder were manually corrected. We followed the guidelines for lemma specification in SAMA, e.g., verbs are cited using the third person masculine singular perfective form. For our example, the CALIMA lemma is *kal∼im*.

4.5 Table Construction

We converted the mapped ECAL entries to a SAMA-like representation (Graff et al., 2009). In SAMA, morphological information is stored in six tables. Three tables specify complex prefixes, complex suffixes and stems. A complex prefix/suffix is a set of prefix/suffix morphemes that are treated as a single database entry, e.g., *wi+Ha+yi* is a complex prefix made of three prefix morphemes. Each complex prefix, complex suffix and stem has a class category which abstract away from all similarly behaving complex affixes and stems. The other three tables specify compatibility across the class categories (prefix-stem, prefix-suffix and stem-suffix). We extracted triples of prefix-stem-suffix and used them to build the six SAMA-like tables. The generated tables are usable by the sama-analyze engine provided as part of SAMA3.1 (Graff et al., 2009). We also added back off mode support for NOUN_PROP.

Prefix/stem/suffix class categories are generated automatically. We identified specific features of the word's stem and affixes to generate specific affix classes that allow for correct coverage expansion. For example, in a complex suffix, the first morpheme is the only one interacting with the stem. As such, there is no need to give each complex suffix its own class category, but rather assign the class category based on the first morpheme. This allows us to automatically extend the coverage of the analyzer compared to that of the ECAL lexicon.

We also go further in terms of generalizations. For instance, some of the pronoun clitics in EGY have two forms that depend on whether the stem ends with vowel-consonant or two consonants, e.g., كتابها *kitAb+hA* 'her book' as opposed to ابنها *Aibn+ahA* 'her son'. This information is used to give the suffixes *+hA* and *+ahA* different class categories that are generalizable to other similarly behaving clitics.

At this stage of our system, which we refer to as CALIMA-core in Section 5.2, there are 252 unique complex prefixes and 550 unique complex suffixes, constructed from 43 and 86 unique simple prefixes and suffixes, respectively. The total number of prefix/suffix class categories is only 41 and 78, respectively.

4.6 Various Table Extensions

We extended the CALIMA-core tables in a similar approach to the extension of SAMA tables done by Salloum and Habash (2011). We distinguish two types of extensions.

Additional Clitics and POS Tags We added a number of clitics and POS tags that are not part of ECAL, e.g., the prepositional clitic +ع *Ea+* 'on' and multiple POS tags for the proclitic +ف *fa+* (as CONJ, SUB_CONJ and CONNEC_PART). Here we copied a related entry and modified it but kept its category class. For example, in the case of +ع *Ea+* 'on', we copied a prepositional clitic with similar distribution and behavior: +ب *bi+* 'with'.

Non-CODA Orthography Support We extended the generated tables to include common non-CODA orthographic variants. The following are some examples of the expansions. First, we added the variant و+ *+w* for two suffixes: ه+ *+uh* 'his/him' and وا+ *+uwA* 'they/you [plural]'. Second, we added the form *ha+* for the future particle *Ha+*. Third, we introduced non-CODA-compliant Hamza forms as variants for some stems. Finally, some of the extensions target specific stems of frequently used words, such as the adverb برضه *brDh* 'also' which can be written as برده *brdh* and برضو *brDw* among other forms. The non-CODA forms are only used to match on the input word, with the returned analysis being a *corrected* analysis. For example, the word هيكتبو *hyktbw* returns the analysis حيكتبوا *HyktbwA* Ha/FUT_PART+yi/IV3P+ktib/IV+uwA/3P 'they will write' among other analyses. The orthographic variations supported include 16 prefix cases, 41 stem cases, and eight suffix cases.

After all the clitic, POS tag and orthographic extensions, the total number of complex prefix entries substantially increases from 352 to 2,421, and the number of complex suffix entries increases from 826 to 1,179. The number of stem entries increases from around 60K to 100K. The total number of recognizable word forms increases from 4M to 48M. We will refer to the system with all the extensions as CALIMA in Section 5.

5 Current Status

In this section, we present some statistics on the current status of the CALIMA analyzer. As with all work on morphological analyzers, there are always ways to improve the quality and coverage.

5.1 System Statistics

CALIMA has 100K stems corresponding to 36K lemmas. There are 2,421 complex prefixes and 1,179 complex suffixes (unique diacritized form and POS tag combinations). The total number of analyzable words by CALIMA is 48M words (compared to the 66K entries in ECAL). This is still limited compared to the SAMA3.1 analyzer (Graff et al., 2009) whose coverage of MSA reaches 246M words. See Table 1.

5.2 Coverage Evaluation

We tested CALIMA against a manually annotated EGY corpus of 3,300 words (Maamouri et al., 2012a) which was not used as part of its development, i.e., a completely blind test.[7] This evaluation is a POS recall evaluation. It is not about selecting the correct POS answer in context. We do not consider whether the diacritization or the lemma choice are correct or not. We compare CALIMA coverage with that of ECAL and a state-of-the-art MSA analyzer, SAMA3.1 (Graff et al., 2009). For the purpose of completeness, we also compare CALIMA-core and an extended version of SAMA3.1. The SAMA3.1 extensions include two EGY verbal proclitics (`Ha/FUT_PART` and `bi/PROG_PART`), some alternative suffixes that have no case or mood, and all the orthographic variations used inside CALIMA. We also compare the performance of different merged versions of SAMA3.1 and CALIMA. The results are presented in Table 1.

The second column in Table 1, *Correct Answer* indicates the percentage of the test words whose correct analysis in context appears among the analyses returned by the analyzer. The third column, *No Correct Answer*, presents the percentage of time one or more analyses are returned, but none matching the correct answer. The fourth column, *No Analysis*, indicates the percentage of words returning no analyses. The last column presents the total number of recognizable words in the system.

CALIMA provides among its results a correct answer for POS tags over 84% of the time. This is almost 27% absolute over the original list of words from ECAL and almost 21% absolute over the SAMA3.1 system. The various extensions in CALIMA give it about 10% absolute over CALIMA-core (and increase its size 10-fold). The limited extensions to SAMA3.1 reduce the difference between it and CALIMA-core by 50% relative. The overall performance of CALIMA-core merged with SAMA3.1 is comparable to CALIMA, although CALIMA has three times the number of no-analysis cases. Merging CALIMA and extended SAMA3.1 increases the performance to 92%, an 8% absolute increase over CALIMA alone. The final rate of no-analysis cases is only 1%.

5.3 Error Analysis

We analyzed a sample of 100 cases where no answer was found (*No Correct Answer + No Analysis*) for CALIMA+extended SAMA3.1. About a third of the cases (30%) are due to gold tag errors. Irrecoverable typographical errors occur 5% of the time, e.g., فين *fyn* instead of في *fy* 'in'. Only 2% of the cases involve a speech effect, e.g., جميييييل *jmyyyyyl* 'beautiful!!!'. A fifth of the cases (22%) involve a non-CODA orthographic choice which was not extended, e.g., the shortened long vowel in حجات *HjAt* instead of the CODA-compliant حاجات *HAjAt* 'things'. Another fifth of the cases (20%) are due to incomplete paradigms, i.e., the lemma exists but not the specific inflected stem. Finally, 21% of the cases receive a SAMA3.1 analysis that is almost correct, except for the presence of some mood/case mark-

[7] We ignore some specific choices made by the annotators, most importantly the use of ".VN" to mark verbal nominals, which is not even supported in SAMA3.1. We also ignore some annotation choices that are not consistent with the latest LDC guidelines (Maamouri et al., 2012b), such as using gender-marked plurals in some contexts, e.g., 3MP instead of 3P.

	Correct Answer	No Correct Answer	No Analysis	Words
ECAL	57.4%	14.7%	27.9%	66K
SAMA3.1	63.7%	27.1%	9.3%	246M
extended SAMA3.1	68.8%	24.9%	6.3%	511M
CALIMA-**core**	73.9%	10.8%	15.3%	4M
CALIMA	84.1%	8.0%	7.9%	48M
CALIMA-**core** + SAMA3.1	84.4%	12.8%	2.8%	287M
CALIMA + **extended** SAMA3.1	92.1%	7.0%	1.0%	543M

Table 1: Comparison of seven morphological analysis systems on a manually annotated test set. The second column indicates the percentage of the test words whose correct analysis in context appears among the analyses returned by the analyzer. The third column presents the percentage of time one or more analyses are returned, but none matching the correct answer. The fourth column indicates the percentage of words returning no analyses. The last column presents the total number of recognizable words in the system.

ers that are absent in EGY, and which we did not handle. Overall, these are positive results that suggest the next steps should involve additional orthographic and morphological extensions and paradigm completion.

6 Outlook

We plan to continue improving the coverage of CALIMA using a variety of methods. First, we are investigating techniques to automatically fill in the paradigm gaps using information from multiple entries in ECAL belonging to different lemmas that share similar characteristics, e.g., hollow verbs in Form I. Another direction is to update our tables with less common orthographic variations, perhaps using information from the phonological forms in ECAL. Manual addition of specific entries will also be considered to fill in lexicon gaps. Furthermore, we plan to add additional features which we did not discuss such as the English and MSA glosses for all the entries in CALIMA. We also plan to make this tool public so it can be used by other people working on EGY NLP tasks, from annotating corpora to building morphological disambiguation tools.

Acknowledgments

This paper is based upon work supported by the Defense Advanced Research Projects Agency (DARPA) under Contract No. HR0011-12-C-0014. Any opinions, findings and conclusions or recommendations expressed in this paper are those of the authors and do not necessarily reflect the views of DARPA. We thank Mohamed Maamouri, Owen Rambow, Seth Kulick, Mona Diab and Mike Ciul, for helpful discussions and feedback.

References

Ernest T. Abdel-Massih, Zaki N. Abdel-Malek, and El-Said M. Badawi. 1979. *A Reference Grammar of Egyptian Arabic*. Georgetown University Press.

Hitham Abo Bakr, Khaled Shaalan, and Ibrahim Ziedan. 2008. A Hybrid Approach for Converting Written Egyptian Colloquial Dialect into Diacritized Arabic. In *The 6th International Conference on Informatics and Systems, INFOS2008*. Cairo University.

Imad Al-Sughaiyer and Ibrahim Al-Kharashi. 2004. Arabic Morphological Analysis Techniques: A Comprehensive Survey. *Journal of the American Society for Information Science and Technology*, 55(3):189–213.

Mohamed Altantawy, Nizar Habash, and Owen Rambow. 2011. Fast Yet Rich Morphological Analysis. In *Proceedings of the 9th International Workshop on Finite-State Methods and Natural Language Processing (FSMNLP 2011)*, Blois, France.

Kenneth Beesley, Tim Buckwalter, and Stuart Newton. 1989. Two-Level Finite-State Analysis of Arabic Morphology. In *Proceedings of the Seminar on Bilingual Computing in Arabic and English*, page n.p.

Tim Buckwalter. 2004. Buckwalter arabic morphological analyzer version 2.0. LDC catalog number LDC2004L02, ISBN 1-58563-324-0.

Tim Buckwalter. 2007. Issues in Arabic Morphological Analysis. In A. van den Bosch and A. Soudi, editors, *Arabic Computational Morphology: Knowledge-based and Empirical Methods*. Springer.

Mark W. Cowell. 1964. *A Reference Grammar of Syrian Arabic*. Georgetown University Press.

Mona Diab, Kadri Hacioglu, and Daniel Jurafsky, 2007. *Arabic Computational Morphology: Knowledge-based and Empirical Methods*, chapter Automated Methods for Processing Arabic Text: From Tokenization to Base Phrase Chunking. Springer.

Wallace Erwin. 1963. *A Short Reference Grammar of Iraqi Arabic*. Georgetown University Press.

Hassan Gadalla, Hanaa Kilany, Howaida Arram, Ashraf Yacoub, Alaa El-Habashi, Amr Shalaby, Krisjanis Karins, Everett Rowson, Robert MacIntyre, Paul Kingsbury, David Graff, and Cynthia McLemore. 1997. CALLHOME Egyptian Arabic Transcripts. In *Linguistic Data Consortium, Philadelphia*.

Hassan Gadalla. 2000. *Comparative Morphology of Standard and Egyptian Arabic*. LINCOM EUROPA.

David Graff, Mohamed Maamouri, Basma Bouziri, Sondos Krouna, Seth Kulick, and Tim Buckwalter. 2009. Standard Arabic Morphological Analyzer (SAMA) Version 3.1. Linguistic Data Consortium LDC2009E73.

Nizar Habash and Owen Rambow. 2005. Arabic Tokenization, Part-of-Speech Tagging and Morphological Disambiguation in One Fell Swoop. In *Proceedings of the 43rd Annual Meeting of the Association for Computational Linguistics (ACL'05)*, pages 573–580, Ann Arbor, Michigan.

Nizar Habash and Owen Rambow. 2006. MAGEAD: A Morphological Analyzer and Generator for the Arabic Dialects. In *Proceedings of the 21st International Conference on Computational Linguistics and 44th Annual Meeting of the Association for Computational Linguistics*, pages 681–688, Sydney, Australia.

Nizar Habash, Abdelhadi Soudi, and Tim Buckwalter. 2007. On Arabic Transliteration. In A. van den Bosch and A. Soudi, editors, *Arabic Computational Morphology: Knowledge-based and Empirical Methods*. Springer.

Nizar Habash, Mona Diab, and Owen Rabmow. 2012. Conventional Orthography for Dialectal Arabic. In *Proceedings of the Language Resources and Evaluation Conference (LREC)*, Istanbul.

Nizar Habash. 2007. Arabic Morphological Representations for Machine Translation. In Antal van den Bosch and Abdelhadi Soudi, editors, *Arabic Computational Morphology: Knowledge-based and Empirical Methods*. Kluwer/Springer.

Nizar Habash. 2010. *Introduction to Arabic Natural Language Processing*. Morgan & Claypool Publishers.

Clive Holes. 2004. *Modern Arabic: Structures, Functions, and Varieties*. Georgetown Classics in Arabic Language and Linguistics. Georgetown University Press.

H. Kilany, H. Gadalla, H. Arram, A. Yacoub, A. El-Habashi, and C. McLemore. 2002. Egyptian Colloquial Arabic Lexicon. LDC catalog number LDC99L22.

George Anton Kiraz. 2000. Multi-Tiered Nonlinear Morphology Using Multi-Tape Finite Automata: A Case Study on Syriac and Arabic. *Computational Linguistics*, 26(1):77–105.

Mohamed Maamouri, Ann Bies, Tim Buckwalter, Mona Diab, Nizar Habash, Owen Rambow, and Dalila Tabessi. 2006. Developing and Using a Pilot Dialectal Arabic Treebank. In *Proceedings of the Language Resources and Evaluation Conference (LREC)*, Genoa, Italy.

Mohamed Maamouri, Ann Bies, Seth Kulick, Dalila Tabessi, and Sondos Krouna. 2012a. Egyptian Arabic Treebank Pilot.

Mohamed Maamouri, Sondos Krouna, Dalila Tabessi, Nadia Hamrouni, and Nizar Habash. 2012b. Egyptian Arabic Morphological Annotation Guidelines.

Emad Mohamed, Behrang Mohit, and Kemal Oflazer. 2012. Annotating and Learning Morphological Segmentation of Egyptian Colloquial Arabic. In *Proceedings of the Language Resources and Evaluation Conference (LREC)*, Istanbul.

Jason Riesa and David Yarowsky. 2006. Minimally Supervised Morphological Segmentation with Applications to Machine Translation. In *Proceedings of the 7th Conference of the Association for Machine Translation in the Americas (AMTA06)*, pages 185–192, Cambridge,MA.

Wael Salloum and Nizar Habash. 2011. Dialectal to Standard Arabic Paraphrasing to Improve Arabic-English Statistical Machine Translation. In *Proceedings of the First Workshop on Algorithms and Resources for Modelling of Dialects and Language Varieties*, pages 10–21, Edinburgh, Scotland.

Otakar Smrž. 2007. *Functional Arabic Morphology. Formal System and Implementation*. Ph.D. thesis, Charles University in Prague, Prague, Czech Republic.

Hindi Derivational Morphological Analyzer

Nikhil Kanuparthi
LTRC
IIIT-Hyderabad
India

Abhilash Inumella
LTRC
IIIT-Hyderabad
India

{nikhil.kvs,abhilashi}@research.iiit.ac.in

Dipti Misra Sharma
LTRC
IIIT-Hyderabad
India
dipti@iiit.ac.in

Abstract

Hindi is an Indian language which is relatively rich in morphology. A few morphological analyzers of this language have been developed. However, they give only inflectional analysis of the language. In this paper, we present our Hindi derivational morphological analyzer. Our algorithm upgrades an existing inflectional analyzer to a derivational analyzer and primarily achieves two goals. First, it successfully incorporates derivational analysis in the inflectional analyzer. Second, it also increases the coverage of the inflectional analysis of the existing inflectional analyzer.

1 Introduction

Morphology is the study of processes of word formation and also the linguistic units such as morphemes, affixes in a given language. It consists of two branches: derivational morphology and inflectional morphology. Derivational morphology is the study of those processes of word formation where new words are formed from the existing stems through the addition of morphemes. The meaning of the resultant new word is different from the original word and it often belongs to a different syntactic category. Example: happiness (noun) = happy (adjective) + ness. Inflectional morphology is the study of those processes of word formation where various inflectional forms are formed from the existing stems. Number is an example of inflectional morphology. Example: cars = car + plural affix 's'.

The main objective of our work is to develop a tool which executes the derivational morphological analysis of Hindi. Morphological analysis is an important step for any linguistically informed natural language processing task. Most morphological analyzers perform only inflectional analysis. However, derivational analysis is also crucial for better performance of several systems. They are used to improve the efficiency of machine translators (C Gdaniec et al., 2001). They are also used in search engines to improve the information extraction (J Vilares et al., 2001). Since derivational processes can often be productive in a language, the development of an effective derivational analyzer will prove beneficial in several aspects.

We developed a derivational analyzer for Hindi over an already existing inflectional analyzer developed at IIIT Hyderabad. In this approach, first, the derived words in Hindi were studied to obtain the derivational suffixes of the language. Then the rules were designed by understanding the properties of the suffixes. The Hindi Wikipedia was also utilized to collect the required background data. Finally, an algorithm was developed based on the above findings. This algorithm has been used to upgrade the inflectional analyzer to a derivational analyzer.

In the sections that follow, we describe the approach we followed to develop our derivational analyzer and the experiments that we conducted using our system.

2 Related Work

There is no derivational morphological analyzer for Hindi to the best of our knowledge. However, a few inflectional morphological analyzers (IIIT; Vishal and G. Singh, 2008; Niraj and Robert, 2010) of this language have been developed. There are derivational analyzers for other Indian languages like Marathi (Ashwini Vaidya, 2009) and Kannada (Bhuvaneshwari C Melinamath et al., 2011). The Marathi morphological analyzer was built using a Paradigm based approach whereas the Kannada analyzer was built using an FST based approach. As far as English is concerned, there are some important works (Woods, 2000; Hoeppner, 1982) pertaining to the area of derivational morphological analysis. However, both of these are lexicon based works.

For our work, we employed a set of suffix replacement rules and a dictionary in our derivational analyzer, having taken insights from the Porter's stemmer (Porter, 1980) and the K-stemmer (R. Krovetz. 1993). They are amongst the most cited stemmers in the literature. The primary goal of Porter's stemmer is suffix stripping. So when a word is given as input, the stemmer strips all the suffixes in the word to produce a stem. It achieves the task in five steps applying rules at each step. Given a word as input, the Krovetz stemmer removes inflectional suffixes present in the word in three steps. First it converts the plural form of the word into a singular form, then it converts past tense to present tense, and finally removes -ing. As the last step, the stemmer checks the dictionary for any recoding and returns the stem. Our algorithm uses the main principles of both the Porters stemmer and Krovetz stemmer. The suffix replacement rules of our algorithm resemble that of the Porters and a segment of the algorithm is analogous to the dictionary based approach of the Krovetzs stemmer.

3 Existing Inflectional Hindi Morphological Analyzers

A derivational morph analyzer can be developed from an existing morph analyzer instead of building one from scratch. So three inflectional analyzers were considered for the purpose. The morphological analyzer developed by Vishal and Gurpreet stores all the commonly used word forms for all Hindi root words in its database. Thus, space is a constraint for this analyzer but the search time is quite low. The morph analyzer developed by Niraj and Robert extracts a set of suffix replacement rules from a corpus and a dictionary. The rules are applied to an inflected word to obtain the root word. They show that the process of developing such rulessets is simple and it can be applied to develop morphological analyzers of other Indian languages.

However, our derivational analyzer is an extension of an existing inflectional morphological analyzer developed at IIIT Hyderabad (Bharati Akshar et al, 1995). The inflectional analyzer is based on the paradigm model. It uses the combination of paradigms and a root word dictionary to provide inflectional analysis. Given an inflected Hindi word, this inflectional analyzer returns its root form and other grammatical features such as gender, number, person, etc. For example: if the input word to the morphological analyzer is *bAgabAnoM*[1] (gardeners), the output will be *bAgabAna* (gardener), noun, m, pl, etc. Here the word *bAgabAna* is the root word of the input word. 'Noun' is the category of the input word, 'm' means masculine and 'pl' means that the input word is plural in number.

The analyzer uses a root word dictionary for the purpose. If a word is present in the root word dictionary, the analyzer handles all the inflections pertaining to that word. For example: *xe* (give) is a root word present in the dictionary of the analyzer. *xewA* (gives), *xenA* (to give), *xiyA* (gave) and other inflectional forms of the root word xe are handled by the analyzer. There are 34407 words in the root word dictionary.

The analyzer handles inflected words using the paradigm tables. Every entry (word) in the dictionary has values like lexical category, paradigm class, etc. For example: there is a word *pulisavAlA* (policeman) in the dictionary. Its paradigm class is *ladakA*. Table 1 shows the paradigm forms of *ladakA*. Since the paradigm value of *pulisavAlA* is *ladakA*, its four inflections will be similar to the four paradigms of *ladakA* (root paradigm). The four inflections of *pulisavAlA* are *pulisavAlA, pulisavAle, pulisavAle, pulisavAloM*. Only the root form (word) *pulisavAlA* is present in the dictionary. In this way every root word present in the dictionary belongs to a paradigm class and this paradigm class has a structured paradigm table containing all the inflections of the main paradigm. This paradigm table is used by

[1]The Hindi words are in wx-format (sanskrit.inria.fr/DATA/wx.html) followed by IIIT-Hyderabad.

Table 1: Paradigm table of *ladakA*

Case	Singular form	Plural form
Direct	*ladakA* (boy)	*ladake* (boys)
Oblique	*ladake* (boy)	*ladakoM* (boys)

the analyzer to reconstruct all the inflections of the root words belonging to this paradigm class. Therefore the analyzer can analyze a word only if its root word is present in the dictionary.

This inflectional morphological analyzer works as a platform for our derivational morphological analyzer. So our tool gives derivational analysis of all the words whose root forms are present in the root word dictionary. Our tool also tackles certain words whose root forms are not present in the root word dictionary of the IIIT morphological analyzer.

4 Approach

We pursued the following five step approach for building our derivational analyzer.

4.1 Studying Hindi Derivations

To build the derivational morphological analyzer, we first conducted a study to identify the derivational suffixes and the related morphological changes. After identifying the suffixes, the rules pertaining to these suffixes were obtained.

First, the nouns present in the Hindi vocabulary were studied. The study of nouns helped us in identifying some of the most productive derivational suffixes present in the language. For example, let us consider the word *maxaxagAra (helper)*. This word is derived from the word *maxaxa* (*maxaxagAra* = *maxaxa (help)* + *gAra*). But gAra cannot be confirmed as a suffix because of just one instance. In order to confirm *gAra* as a suffix, even other words ending with *gAra* must be examined. The more the number of words we find, the greater is the productivity of the suffix. Words like *yAxagAra* (derived from *yAxa*) and *gunAhagAra (criminal)* (derived from *gunAha (crime)*) prove that *gAra* is a derivational suffix. However, every word ending with *gAra* need not be a derived word. For example: the word *aMgAra* is not a derived word. Therefore only relevant words were studied and the suffixes were obtained only from them.

Table 2: Example derivations of some suffixes

Suffix	Root	Derivation
Ana	*laganA*	*lagAna*
bAna	*bAga*	*bAgabAna*
gAra	*yAxa*	*yAxagAra*
xAra	*xukAna*	*xukAnaxAra*
ika	*aXikAra*	*aXikArika*
I	*KuSa*	*KuSI*
AI	*acCA*	*acCAI*

Table 3: Rules of few suffixes

Suffix	First set rules
bAna	noun = noun/adj + *bAna*
gAra	noun = noun/adj + *gAra*
xAra	noun = noun/adj + *xAra*
ika	adj = noun - *a* + *ika*

The entire process of obtaining the derivational suffixes was done manually and was a time consuming process. This process was repeated for adjectives as well. Only those suffixes that participate in the formation of nouns and adjectives were found. A total of 22 productive derivational suffixes were procured. Table 2 shows a few suffixes and their derivations.

4.2 Derivational Rules

After finding the derivational suffixes, two sets of derivational rules were developed for each suffix. The first set explains the formation of the derived words from their root words. Let us consider the suffix *gAra*. This suffix generates nouns from nouns and adjectives. The rule of this suffix explains the formation of derivations like *yAxagAra* (*yAxagAra* = *yAxa* (noun) + *gAra*) and *maxaxagAra* (*maxaxagAra* = *maxaxa* + *gAra*). The second set consists of reverse rules of the first set. The reverse rule for the previous example is noun/adj = noun - suffix. In this way, rules were developed for all the 22 derivational suffixes. These rules form a vital component of our algorithm. Table 3 contains the derivational rules of a few suffixes.

4.3 Finding Majority Properties

The majority properties (of derived words of a suffix) are the properties which most of the words exhibit. Example: let us consider the derived words of the suffix *vAlA*. There are 36 derived words of the *vAlA* suffix in the root word dictionary. Some of these words are adjectives but the majority are nouns. Hence noun is fixed as the category (majority category) for derived words of this class. Similarly the majority paradigm class of these words is *ladakA*. The majority properties of derived words pertaining to all the 22 suffixes were acquired.

The majority properties of a suffix help us in the derivational analysis of the unknown derived words of that suffix. For example: consider the word *GaravAlA (housekeeper)*. Let us assume that it is not present in the root word dictionary. Therefore the lexical category, paradigm value and other important features of this word are not known. But let us assume that this word is a genuine derived word of the suffix *vAlA*. So the tool must handle this case. The majority properties of the *vAlA* suffix are assigned to this word. So noun and *ladakA* are fixed as the category and paradigm of this word. Thus the genuine derived words which are unknown to the analyzer will be analyzed using the majority properties.

The majority properties of derived words were obtained in two main steps. First, a suffix was considered. Then all the derived words pertaining to that suffix were acquired. Only genuine derived words were taken into consideration. Genuine derivations were found out using the suffix derivational rules. Example: let us take the word *maxaxagAra* (ending with *gAra*). First, the root word of this word is retrieved using the *gAra* derivational rule. The root word according to the rule is *maxaxa*. This word is present in the dictionary and it also satisfies the category condition of the rule. The word *maxaxa* is a noun. Hence the word *maxaxagAra* is accepted as a derived word. If the word *maxaxa* is not found in the dictionary or if its category is not a noun/adjective, the word *maxaxagAra* will be rejected. In this way all the valid derivations of the suffix were acquired. This process was repeated for other suffixes as well. In the second step, the majority properties of the derived words were directly retrieved.

Finally, a suffix table was built using the majority properties of the derived words. The suffix table contains all the suffixes and their inflectional forms. Table 4 contains few suffixes and their inflectional forms. For example: the majority paradigm of derived words of *vAlA* suffix is *ladakA*. This implies that the derived words of this suffix end with *vAlA*, *vAle* and *vAloM*. Thus the possible inflections of a suffix can be derived from its majority properties. This information was stored in a table. The majority properties and the suffix table play an important role in the analysis of the unknown words. Their usage in our algorithm will be described in the later sections.

Table 4: Few suffixes and their forms

Suffix	Suffix-forms
Ana	*Ana*
bAna	*bAna, bAnoM*
gAra	*gAra, gAroM*
xAra	*xAra, xAroM*
ika	*ika*
I	*I*
AI	*AI*
anI	*anI, aniyAz, aniyoM*

4.4 Using Wikipedia Data for Confirming Genuineness

If an invalid word is not analyzed by the inflectional analyzer, there is no need for proceeding to the derivational analysis of that word. Therefore the genuineness of a word must be tested before going for the derivational analysis. The Hindi Wikipedia was chosen as a resource that enables us to test the genuineness of a word.

A total of 400k words were extracted from the Hindi Wikipedia. This data contains many words which do not exist in Hindi vocabulary. So 220k proper Hindi words were selected (on the basis of frequency) from the data and a list containing those 220k words was created. A word will be treated as a genuine word only when it is present in that list. This assumption is used by our algorithm. The Wiki data is used as a standard corpus.

4.5 Algorithm for Derivational Analysis

An algorithm was developed to make use of the existing inflectional morphological analyzer for derivational analysis. This algorithm enabled us to bypass the construction of a derivational analyzer from the scratch. The majority properties of the derivations, the Wikipedia data and the suffix-table are also employed by the algorithm for analyzing unknown derivations.

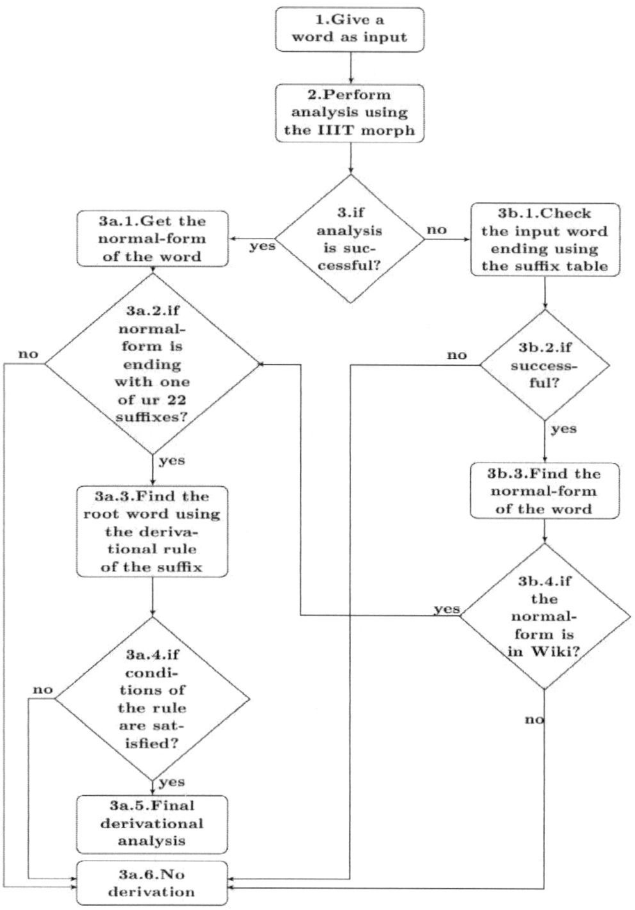

Figure 1: Algorithm

The input to the algorithm is a word. The output is a combination of the inflectional analysis and the derivational analysis of the input word. For example: if the input word is *bAgabAnoM* (gardeners). First, the algorithm gives the inflectional analysis of the input word. In this case the word *bAgabAnoM* is a noun, plural in number, etc. Then it gives the information (category, gender) of the root word (*bAga* (garden)) from which the input word is derived (derivational analysis). So a dual analysis of the input word is provided.

4.6 Examples

The following 4 examples explain the working of the algorithm in 4 different cases. These examples are provided to give a clear picture of the complete algorithm.

a) Example 1

Input word: ***pulisavAle* (Policemen)**

In the step-2, the word is analyzed by the IIIT inflectional analyzer. In the step 3a.1, the word *pulisavAlA* (Policeman) is the normal-form of the input word. The normal-form is ending (*vAlA*) with one of our 22 suffixes. The rule of the suffix is noun = noun/verb + *vAlA*. So the root word is *pulisa* because *pulisavAlA* ≐ *pulisa* + *vAlA*. The word *pulisa* should be a noun or a verb in order to satisfy the rule. All the conditions are met and the step 3a.5 becomes the vital final step. This step gives the information that the final root word *pulisa* is a masculine noun and the input word is also a masculine noun and it is plural in number. Here the information about the final root word and the input word is again given using the inflectional morphological analyzer.

b) Example 2

Input word: ***kirAexAroM* (Tenants)**

The IIIT inflectional analyzer cannot analyze this word. The word *kirAexAroM* is ending with one of the forms (*xAroM*) present in the suffix table. The normal-form of the input word is obtained by replacing the suffix form in the input word with the suffix. Hence the normal-form of the input word *kirAexAroM* is *kirAexAra*. In this way, the normal-form of the input word is acquired without the inflectional analyzer. The word *kirAexAra* is present in Wiki data and it is ending with one of the 22 suffixes. The rule of the suffix is noun = noun/adj + *xAra*. So the root word is *kirAe* because *kirAexAra* = *kirAe* + *xAra*.

c) Example 3

Input word: ***ladake* (Boys)**

In the step-2, the word is analyzed by the IIIT inflectional analyzer. The normal form of the word is *ladakA* (boy). The normal-form of the word is not ending with any of our 22 suffixes. So there is no derivational analysis of this particular case.

d) Example 4

Input word: ***ppppwA* (invalid word)**

The IIIT inflectional analyzer cannot analyze this word. The word *ppppwA* is ending with one of the forms (*wA*) present in the suffix table. But the normal-form (*ppppwA*) is not present in Wikipedia. So there is no derivational analysis for this particular case.

4.7 Expanding Inflectional Analysis

The algorithm for derivational analysis was also used for expanding the inflectional analysis of the analyzer. Consider the second example in the previous section. The word *kirAexAroM* is analyzed by the derivational analyzer even though its root form (*kirAexAra*) is not present in the root word dictionary. Words like *kirAexAra* are genuine derivations and can be added to the root word dictionary. The addition of such kind of words will extend the inflectional analysis of the analyzer. For example. if the word *kirAexAra* is added, its forms *kirAexAroM* and *kirAexAra* will be automatically analyzed. This is because the word *kirAexAra* would be added along with its features/values like category, paradigm class, etc.

Therefore all the words which fall into the example-2 category of the previous section can be added to the dictionary. All such words must be obtained in order to expand our dictionary. For this purpose, a Wiki data consisting of 220k Wiki words was extracted from Wikipedia. Out of these 220k words, 40k words are ending with our 22 suffixes and their forms. So the derived words which can be analyzed by our system are part of this sub-dataset. Out of 40k words, the derivational analyzer analyzed 5579 words. The inflectional analyzer analyzed only 2362 words out of 40000. So the derivational analyzer analyzed 3217 derived words more than the inflectional analyzer. So these words were added to the root word dictionary for expanding the inflectional analysis of the analyzer. The algorithm which was designed to perform derivational analysis also inflated the inflectional analysis of the analyzer.

5 Experiments and Results

The performance of our derivational analyzer must be compared with an existing derivational analyzer. Since there is no such derivational analyzer, we compared the performance of our tool with the existing IIIT inflectional analyzer (or the old morphological analyzer). The two tools must be tested on a gold-data (data that does not contain any errors). For example: let us assume that we have a data of 100 words and their morphological analysis. The analysis of these 100 words does not contain any errors and it is a gold-data. Now we must get the analysis of these 100 words from both the derivational analyzer and the old morphological analyzer. Then their analyses must be compared against the gold-data. This is nothing but directly comparing the outputs of the derivational analyzer and the old morphological analyzer. This will help in evaluating the derivational analyzer. This method of evaluation will also tell the improvement the derivational analyzer achieved.

Type	*Output / Gold*	*Description*
Type 1	ABCD / ABCD	All the analyses present in the reference present in the output + No wrong analyses present in the output
Type 2	ABCDE / ABCD	All the analyses present in the reference present in the output + Some wrong analyses present in the output
Type 3	ABC / ABCD	Some analyses present in the reference present in the output + No wrong analyses present in the output
Type 4	ABCE / ABCD	Some analyses present in the reference present in the output + Some wrong analyses present in the output
Type 5	EFG / ABCD	No analyses present in the reference present in the output + Some wrong analyses present in the output
Type 6	No Output / ABCD	No output given by the morph

Figure 2: Evaluation Methodology for Morph Analyzers

The figure 2 (Amba P Kulkarni, 2010) explains our evaluation methodology for morphological analyzers. Let us continue with the example mentioned in the previous paragraph. First, we find the analysis of the 100 words by the old morph analyzer. We compare its output with the gold output/analysis. Let there be 50 words which belong to Type-1. It means the gold analysis and morphological analysis (by old morph) of 50 words is perfectly equal. Let there be 10 words which belong to Type-6. It means

Table 5: Output analysis of old morph analyzer

Type	Number of instances	% of Type
Type1	*2361*	*47.2*
Type2	*763*	*15.2*
Type3	*419*	*8.4*
Type4	*575*	*11.5*
Type5	*599*	*11.9*
Type6	*288*	*5.8*

Table 6: Output analysis of derivational analyzer

Type	Number of instances	% of Type
Type1	*2600*	*51.9*
Type2	*771*	*15.4*
Type3	*418*	*8.4*
Type4	*576*	*11.5*
Type5	*609*	*12.2*
Type6	*31*	*0.6*

that the old morphological analyzer could not analyze 10 words but there is gold analysis of those words. In this way, each type forms an important part of the evaluation process. Similarly we evaluate the analysis of the 100 words by the derivational analyzer. Finally we compare the evaluations of the old morphological analyzer and our derivational analyzer. This is our evaluation methodology.

So a gold-data consisting of the analysis of 5000 words was taken. The linguistic experts of IIIT Hyderabad have built this data and it was acquired from that institution. The 5000 words were tested on both the derivational analyzer and the inflectional analyzer.

Both the analyzers were tested on the gold-data containing 5000 words. The table 6 proves that the performance of the new derivational analyzer is better than the old morphological analyzer. The old analyzer could not provide any output of 288 words (Type-6) whereas that number is only 31 incase of the derivational analyzer. As a result of this improvement, the overall Type-1 (Perfect output which is completely matching with the gold output) of derivational analyzer is nearly 5% more than that of the old morphological analyzer. The data size is small (only 5000). A testing on a larger gold-data will show an even better picture of the improvement that can be achieved by the derivational analyzer.

6 Conclusions

We presented an algorithm which uses an existing inflectional analyzer for performing derivational analysis. The algorithm uses the main principles of both the Porters stemmer and Krovetz stemmer for achieving the task. The algorithm achieves decent precision and recall. It also expands the coverage of the inflectional analyzer. But it must be incorporated in applications like machine translators which use derivational analysis for understanding its real strengths and limitations.

References

Claudia Gdaniec, Esm Manandise, Michael C. McCord. 2001. *Derivational morphology to the rescue: how it can help resolve unfound words in MT*, pp.129–131. Summit VIII: Machine Translation in the Information Age, Proceedings, Santiago de Compostela, Spain.

Jesus Vilares, David Cabrero and Miguel A. Alonso. 2001. *Applying Productive Derivational Morphology to Term Indexing of Spanish Texts.* In Proceedings of CICLing.

Vishal Goyal, Gurpreet Singh Lehal. 2008. *Hindi Morphological Analyzer and Generator*, pp. 1156–1159. IEEE Computer Society Press, California, USA.

Niraj Aswani, Robert Gaizauskas. 2010. *Developing Morphological Analysers for South Asian Languages: Experimenting with the Hindi and Gujarati Languages.* In Proceedings of LREC.

Ashwini Vaidya. 2009. *Using paradigms for certain morphological phenomena in Marathi.* In Proceedings of ICON.

Bhuvaneshwari C Melinamath, Shubhagini D. 2011. *A robust Morphological analyzer to capture Kannada noun Morphology*, VOL 13. IPCSIT.

William A. Woods. 2000. *Aggressive Morphology for Robust Lexical Coverage.* In Proceedings of ANLC.

Wolfgang Hoeppner. 1982. *A multilayered approach to the handling of word formation.* In Proceedings of COLING.

R. Krovetz. 1993. *Viewing morphology as an inference process.* In Proceedings of COLING.

M. F. Porter. 1980. *An algorithm for suffix stripping.* Originally published in Program, 14 no. 3, pp 130-137.

Bharati Akshar, Vineet Chaitanya, Rajeev Sangal. 1995. *Natural Language Processing: A Paninian Perspective.* Prentice-Hall of India.

Amba P Kulkarni. 2010. *A Report on Evaluation of Sanskrit Tools.*

Phrase-Based Approach for Adaptive Tokenization

Jianqiang Ma
Department of Linguistics
University of Tübingen
Wilhelmstr. 19, Tübingen, 72074, Germany
jma@sfs.uni-tuebingen.de

Dale Gerdemann
Department of Linguistics
University of Tübingen
Wilhelmstr. 19, Tübingen, 72074, Germany
dg@sfs.uni-tuebingen.de

Abstract

Fast re-training of word segmentation models is required for adapting to new resources or domains in NLP of many Asian languages without word delimiters. The traditional tokenization model is efficient but inaccurate. This paper proposes a phrase-based model that factors sentence tokenization into phrase tokenizations, the dependencies of which are also taken into account. The model has a good OOV recognition ability, which improves the overall performance significantly. The training is a linear time phrase extraction and MLE procedure, while the decoding is via dynamic programming based algorithms.

1 Introduction

In many Asian languages, including Chinese, a sentence is written as a character sequence without word delimiters, thus word segmentation remains a key research topic in language processing for these languages. Although many reports from evaluation tasks present quite positive results, a fundamental problem for real word applications is that most systems heavily depend on the data they were trained on. In order to utilize increasingly available language resources such as user contributed annotations and web lexicon and/or to dynamically construct models for new domains, we have to either frequently re-build models or rely on techniques such as incremental learning and transfer learning, which are unsolved problems themselves.

In the case of frequent model re-building, the most efficient approach is the *tokenization model* (using the terminology in Huang et al., 2007), in which the re-training is just the update of the dictionary and the segmentation is a *greedy* string matching procedure using the dictionary and some disambiguation heuristics, e.g. Liang (1986) and Wang et al. (1991). An extension of this approach is the *dynamic programming* search of the most probable word combination on the *word lattice*, such as Ma (1996) and Sproat et al. (1996), which utilize information such as word frequency statistics in a corpus to build the model and are less efficient but more accurate.

However, all the methods mentioned above are mostly based on the knowledge of in-vocabulary words and usually suffer from poor performance, as the out-of-vocabulary words (OOV) rather than segmentation ambiguities turn out to the dominant error source for word segmentation on real corpora (Huang and Zhao, 2007). This fact has led to a shift of the research focus to modeling the roles of individual characters in the word formation process to tackle the OOV problem. Xue (2003) proposes a *character classification model*, which classifies characters according to their positions in a word using the maximum entropy classifier (Berger et al., 1996). Peng et al. (2004) has further extended this model to its sequential form, i.e. sequence labeling, by adopting linear-chain conditional random fields (CRFs, Lafferty et al., 2001). As it is capable of capturing the morphological behaviors of characters, the character classification model has significantly better performance in OOV recognition and overall segmentation accuracy, and has been the state-of-art since its introduction, suggested by the leading performances of systems based on it in recent international Chinese word segmentation bakeoffs (Emerson, 2005; Levow, 2006; Zhao and Liu, 2010).

The tokenization model has advantages in **simplicity** and **efficiency**, as the basic operation in segmentation is *string matching* with *linear time complexity* to the sentence length and it only needs a dictionary thus requires *no* training as in the character classification model, which can easily have millions of features and require hundreds of iterations in the training phase. On the other hand, it has inferior performance, caused by its poor OOV induction ability.

This work proposes a framework called **phrase-based tokenization** as a generalization of the tokenization model to cope with its deficiencies in OOV recognition, while preserving its advantages of simplicity and efficiency, which are important for adaptive word segmentation. The segmentation hypothesis unit is extended from a *word* to a *phrase*, which is a character string of arbitrary length, i.e. combinations of partial and/or complete words. And the statistics of different tokenizations of the same phrase are collected and used for parameters estimation, which leads to a *linear time* model construction procedure. This extension makes hypothesis units capable of capturing richer context and describing morphological behavior of characters, which improves OOV recognition. Moreover, *overlapping* hypothesis units can be combined once certain consistency conditions are satisfied, which avoids the unrealistic assumption of independence among the tokenizations of neighboring phrases.

Phrase-based tokenization decomposes the sentence tokenization into phrase tokenizations. We use a graph called *phrase tokenization lattice* to represent all the hypotheses of phrase tokenization in a given sentence. Under such a formulation, tokenizing a sentence is transformed to the shortest path search problem on the graph, which can be efficiently solved by dynamic programming techniques similar to the Viterbi (1967) algorithm.

2 Phrase-Based Model

The hypothesis unit of the tokenization model is the *word*, i.e. it selects the best word sequence from all the words that can be matched by substrings of the sentence (usually in a greedy manner). Once a word is chosen, the corresponding boundaries are determined. This implies that as the characters in a word are always considered as a whole, the morphological behavior of an individual character, e.g. the distribution of its positions in words, is ignored thus makes it impossible to model the word formation process and recognize OOV.

Critical tokenization (Guo, 1997) suggests a method of discovering all and only unambiguous token boundaries (critical points) and generating longest substrings with all inner positions ambiguous (critical fragments) under the assumption of *complete dictionary*. Then an *example-based* method using the context can be adopted to disambiguate the tokenization of critical fragments (Hu et al, 2004). However, the complete dictionary assumption is *not* realistic in practice, as the word formation is so dynamic and productive that there is no dictionary that is even close to the complete lexicon. Given the presence of OOV, a word, including a monosyllabic word, in the original dictionary may be a substring, i.e. a *partial word*, of an OOV. In this case, the critical points found by the dictionary are *not* guaranteed to be unambiguous.

As the complete dictionary does not exist as a static object, a possible solution is to make a dynamic dictionary, which induces words on the fly. But this will not be discussed in this paper. Instead, we attempt to generalize the tokenization model to work *without* the complete dictionary. Different from making distinctions of critical fragments and "non-critical" fragments in critical tokenization, we suggest using *phrases* to represent potentially ambiguous fragments of sentences in a unified way. We define a phrase as a substring of a sentence, the boundaries of which, depending on the tokenization, may or may not necessarily match word boundaries. The fact that partial words, including single characters, may appear on both ends of a phrase makes it possible to describe "morphemes in the context" for OOV induction. A consequence of introducing phrase in tokenization is that a manually segmented corpus is needed in order to collect phrases.

2.1 Tokenization

Tokenization is the process of separating words or word-like units from sentences or character strings. We can consider sentence tokenization as a mapping from each position in the sentence to a binary value, which indicates the presence (denoted as #) or the absence of word boundary (denoted as $) at that position. A specific tokenization realization of a sentence can be represented by a list of binary values, which can be generated by the concatenations of its sub-lists. In other words, a tokenization of a given sentence can be represented as the *concatenation* of the tokenizations of its component phrases.

If we assume that the tokenization of a phrase is *independent* of other phrases in the same sentence, the sentence tokenization problem is decomposed to smaller phrase tokenization problems, which are unrelated to each other. The independency assumption is not necessarily true but in general is a good approximation. We take this assumption by default, unless there exists evidence that suggests otherwise. In that case, we introduce a method called *backward dependency match* to fix the problem, which will be discussed in Section 3.3.

2.2 Phrase Tokenization Lattice

Informally a **phrase tokenization lattice**, or *lattice* in short, is a set of hypothesized tokenization of phrases in the given sentence, which is a compact representation of all the possible tokenization for that sentence. Using the notations in Mohri (2002), we formally define a **lattice** as a *weighted directed graph* $<V,E>$ with a mapping $W:E \mapsto A$, where V is the set of *nodes*, E is the set of *edges*, and the mapping W assigns each edge a *weight* w from the semiring $<A,\oplus,\otimes,\bar{0},\bar{1}>$ [1].

For a given sentence $S[0...m]$, each node $v \in V$, denotes a *sentence position* (the position between a pair of adjacent characters in a untokenized sentence). Each edge $e \in E$ from node v_a to node v_b, denotes a tokenization of the phrase between the positions defined by v_a and v_b. And for each edge e, a weight w is determined by the mapping W, denotes the *phrase tokenization probability*, the probability of the phrase defined by the two nodes of the edge being tokenized as the tokenization defined by that edge. A *path* π in the lattice is a sequence of consecutive edges, i.e. $\pi = e_1 e_2 ... e_k$, where e_i and e_{i+1} are connected with a node. The *weight* for the path π can be defined as:

$$w(\pi) = \bigotimes_{i=1}^{k} w(e_i) \qquad (1)$$

which is the product of the weights of its component edges. A path from the source node to the sink node, represents a *tokenization* of the sentence *being factored as the concatenation of tokenizations* of phrases represented by those edges of on that path.

For example, with some edges being pruned, the lattice for the sentence 有人质疑他 'Someone questions him' is shown in Figure 1.

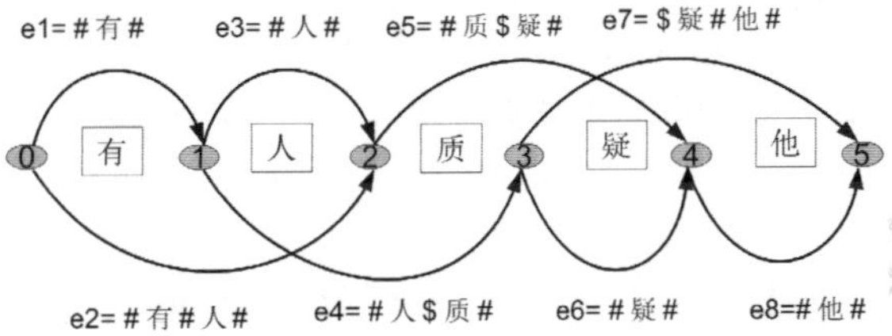

Figure 1. A pruned phrase tokenization lattice. Edges are tokenizations of phrases, e.g. e_5 represents tokenizing 质疑 'question' into a word and e_7 represents tokenizing 疑他 'doubt him' into a partial word 疑 'doubt' followed by a word 他 'him'.

2.3 Tokenization as the Best Path Search

After the introduction of the lattice, we formally describe the tokenization (disambiguation) problem as the best path searching on the lattice:

$$\hat{T} = \arg\max_{T \in D} w(T) \qquad (2)$$

where D is the set of all paths from the source node to the sink node, and $\hat{T}$ is the path with the highest weight, which represents the best tokenization of the sentence. Intuitively, we consider the *product* of phrase tokenization probabilities as the probability of the sentence tokenization that is generated from the concatenation of these phrase tokenizations.

Note that every edge in the lattice is from a node represents an earlier sentence position to a node that represents a later one. In other words, the lattice is *acyclic* and has a clear topological order.

[1] A semiring defines an algebra system with certain rules to compute path probabilities and the max probabilities from a node to another. See Mohri (2002) for details.

In this case, the best path can be found using the Viterbi (1967) algorithm efficiently[2].

3 Training and Inference Algorithms

3.1 Model Training

In order to use the lattice to tokenize unseen sentences, we first have to build a model that can generate the edges and their associated weight, i.e. the tokenization of all the possible phrases and their corresponding phrase tokenization probability. We do it by collecting all the phrases that have occurred in a training corpus and use *maximum likelihood estimation* (MLE) to estimate the phrase tokenization probabilities. The estimation of the probability that a particular phrase $A = a_1 a_2 ..a_n$ being tokenized as the tokenization $T = t_1 t_2 ..t_m$ is given in equation (3), where $C(\bullet)$ represents the empirical count, and the set of all T' stands for all possible tokenizations of A. To avoid extreme cases in which there is no path at all, techniques such as *smoothing* can be applied.

$$P(T \mid A) = \frac{C(T,A)}{\sum_{T'} C(T',A)} = \frac{C(T,A)}{C(A)} \quad (3)$$

The result of the MLE estimation is stored in a data structure called phase tokenization table, from which one can retrieval all the possible tokenizations with their corresponding probabilities for the every phrase that has occurred in the training corpus. With this model, we can construct the lattice, i.e. determine the set of edges E and the mapping function W (defining nodes is trivial) for a given sentence in a simple string matching and table retrieval manner: when a substring of sentence is matched to a stored phrase, an edge is built from the its starting and ending node to represent a tokenization of that phrase, with the weight of the edge equals to the MLE estimation of the stored phrase-tokenization pair.

3.2 Simple Dynamic Programming

Once the model is built, we can tokenize a given sentence by the inference on the lattice which represents that sentence. The proposed simple dynamic programming algorithm (**Algorithm 1**, as shown in Figure 2) can be considered as the phrase tokenization lattice version of the *evalUtterance* algorithm in Venkataraman (2001). The best tokenization of the partial sentence up to a certain position is yielded by the best combination of one previous best tokenization and one of the phrase tokenizations under consideration at the current step.

The upper bound of the time complexity of Algorithm 1 is $O(kn^2)$, where n is the sentence length and k is the maximum number of the possible tokenization for a phrase. But in practice, it is neither necessary nor possible (due to data sparseness) to consider phrases of arbitrary length, so we set a constraint of maximum phrase length of about 10, which makes the time complexity de-facto linear.

Algorithm 1: Simple Dynamic Programming

```
Prerequisite: Phrase Tokenization Table (PT)
Input: Sentence S[0...N]
Initialization:
BestScore= N-dimension zero vector
BestTokenization= N-dimension null-string vector
Algorithms:
for i=1 to N do :            // i: current position in the sentence
    for j=i-1 to 0 do :      // j: starting position of the last phrase
      phrase=S[j:i]
      if phrase in PT :
          tokenization=GetTopTokenization(PT, phrase)
          tokenization_prob=GetProbability(PT, tokenization)
          score=BestScore[j] * tokenization_prob

          if score>BestScore[i] :
              BestTokenization[i]=tokenization
              BestScore[i]=score
              back_pointer[i]=j
      else:
          break   // if the phrase not in PT, exist the inner loop

BestPath ← Path traced back from back_pointer[N]
SentenceTokenization← Concatenation of the BestTokenizaiton
entries of the edges on the BestPath (which are phrase tokenizations)
Output: SentenceTokenization
```

Figure 2. The pseudo code of Algorithm 1.

The key difference to a standard word-lattice based dynamic programming lies in the phrase lattice representation that the algorithm runs on. Instead of representing a word candidate as in Venkataraman (2001), each edge now represents a

[2] More rigid mathematical descriptions of this family of problems and generic algorithms based on semirings are discussed in Mohri (2002) and Huang (2008).

tokenization of a phrase defined by two nodes of the edge, which can include full and partial words. The combination of phrase tokenizations may yield new words that are not in the dictionary, i.e. our method can recognize OOVs.

Let us consider a slightly modified version of the lattice in Figure 1. Suppose edge e_5 =#质$疑# does not exist , i.e. the word 质疑 'question' is not in the dictionary, and there is new edge $e_5' =$ #质$ that links node 2 and node 3 and represents a partial word. Two of possible tokenizations of the sentence are path $p_1 = e_1e_4e_6e_8$ and path $p_2 = e_2e_5'e_7$. Note that p_2 recognizes the word 质疑 'question' by combining two partial words, even though the word itself has not seen before. Of course, this OOV is finally recognized only if a path that can yield it is the best path found by the decoding algorithm.

Once the best path is found, the procedure of mapping it back to segmented words is as follows. The phrase tokenizations represented by the edges of the best path are concatenated, before substituting meta symbols # and $ into white space and empty string, respectively. For example, if $p_2 = e_2e_5'e_7$ is the best path, the concatenation of the phrase tokenizations of the three edges on the path will be #有#人##质$$疑#他#, and removal of $ and substitution of # into the white space will further transform it into 有 人 质疑 他 'Somebody questions him', which is the final result of the algorithm.

3.3 Compatibility and Backward Dependency Match

As mentioned in Section 2, the independency assumption of phrase tokenization is not always true. Considering the example in Figure 1, e_4 and and e_7 are not really *compatible*, as e_4 represents a word while e_7 represents a partial word that expects the suffix of its preceding phrase to form a word with its prefix. To solve this problem, we require that the last (meta) symbol of the preceding tokenization must equal to the first (meta) symbol of the following tokenization in order to concatenate the two. This, however, has the consequence that there may be no valid tokenization at all for some positions. As a result, we have to maintain the top k hypotheses and use the *k-best* path search algorithms instead of 1-best (Mohri, 2002). We adopt the naïve k-best path search, but it is possible to use more advanced techniques (Huang and Chiang, 2005).

The compatibility problem is just the most salient example of the general problem of variable independency assumptions, which is the "unigram model" of phrase tokenization. A natural extension is a higher order Markov model. But that is inflexible, as it assumes a fixed variable dependency structure (the current variable is always dependent on previous n variables). So we propose a method called *backward dependency match*, in which we start from the independency assumption, then try to explore the longest sequence of adjacent dependencies that we can reach via string match for a given phrase and its precedent.

To simplify the discussion, we use sequence labeling, or conditional probability notation of the tokenization. A tokenization of the given character sequence (sentence) is represented as a specific label sequence of same length. The label can be those in the standard 4-tag set of word segmentation (Huang and Zhao, 2007) or the #/$ labels indicating the presence or absence of a word boundary after a specific character.

The possible tokenizations of character sequence $a_1a_2a_3$ are represented as the probability distribution $P(t_1t_2t_3 \mid a_1a_2a_3)$, where $t_1t_2t_3$ are labels of $a_1a_2a_3$. If a tokenization hypothesis of $a_1a_2a_3$ decomposes its tokenization into the concatenation of the tokenization of a_1a_2 and the tokenization of a_3, this factorization can be expressed as $P(t_1t_2 \mid a_1a_2) \times P(t_3 \mid a_3)$, as shown in Figure 3a. For a specific *assignment* $<\overline{a_1}\,\overline{a_2}\,\overline{a_3};\overline{t_1}\,\overline{t_2}\,\overline{t_3}>$, if we find that $<\overline{a_2}\,\overline{a_3}>$ can be tokenized as $<\overline{t_2}\,\overline{t_3}>$, it suggests that t_3 may be *dependent on* a_2 and t_2 as well, so we update the second part of the factorization (at least for this assignment) to: $P(t_3 \mid a_3; a_2t_2)$, which can be estimated as:

$$P(\overline{t_3} \mid \overline{a_3}; \overline{a_2}\,\overline{t_2}) = \frac{C(\overline{a_2}\,\overline{a_3}\,\overline{t_2}\,\overline{t_3})}{\sum_{t_3} C(\overline{a_2}\,\overline{a_3}\,\overline{t_2}\,t_3)} \quad (4)$$

In this case, the factorization of the tokenization $P(t_1t_2t_3 \mid a_1a_2a_3)$ is $P(t_1t_2 \mid a_1a_2) \times P(t_3 \mid a_3;a_2t_2)$, as shown in Figure 3b.

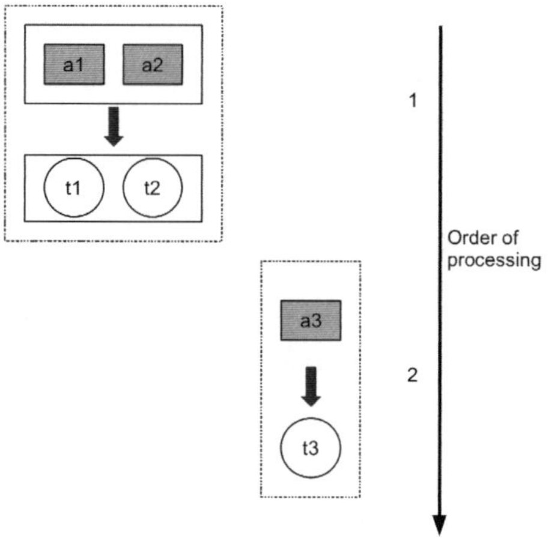

Figure 3a. The factorization of $P(t_1t_2t_3 \mid a_1a_2a_3)$ into $P(t_1t_2 \mid a_1a_2) \times P(t_3 \mid a_3)$.

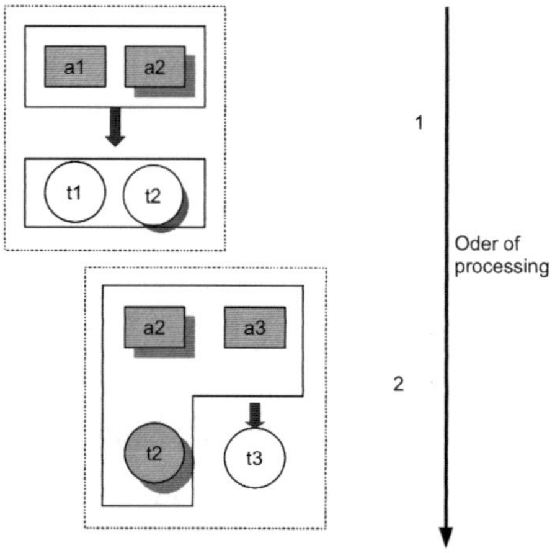

Figure 3b. The factorization of $P(t_1t_2t_3 \mid a_1a_2a_3)$ into $P(t_1t_2 \mid a_1a_2) \times P(t_3 \mid a_3;a_2t_2)$. Note that in the 2nd factor, in addition to a_3, a_2 and t_2 are also observed variables and all of them are treated as a unit (shown by the L-shape). The shadowed parts (a_2 and t_2) represent the matched items.

Algorithm 2 is based on the k-best search algorithm, which calls the backward dependency match after a successful compatibility check, and match as far as possible to get the largest probability of each tokenization hypothesis. In extreme cases, where no tokenization hypothesis survives the compatibility check, the algorithm backs off to Algorithm 1.

4 Experiments

We use the training and testing sets from the second international Chinese word segmentation bakeoff (Emerson, 2005), which are freely available and most widely used in evaluations. There are two corpora in simplified Chinese provided by Peking University (PKU) and Microsoft Research (MSR) and two corpora in traditional Chinese provided by Academic Sinica (AS) and the City University of Hong Kong (CityU). The experiments are conducted in a closed-test manner, in which no extra recourse other than the training corpora is used. We use the same criteria and the official script for evaluation from the bakeoff, which measure the overall segmentation performance in terms of *F-scores*, and the OOV recognition capacity in terms of *Roov*.

Precision is defined as the number of correctly segmented words divided by the total number of words in the segmentation result, where the correctness of the segmented words is determined by matching the segmentation with the gold standard test set. Recall is defined as the number of correctly segmented words divided by the total number of words in the gold standard test set. The evenly-weighted F-score is calculated by:

$$F = 2 \times p \times r / (p + r) \tag{5}$$

Roov is the recall of all the OOV words. And *Riv* is the recall of words that have occurred in the training corpus. The evaluation in this experiment is done automatically using the script provided with the second bakeoffs data.

We have implemented both Algorithm 1 and Algorithm 2 in Python with some simplifications, e.g. only processing phrase up to the length of 10 characters, ignoring several important details such as pruning. The performances are compared with the baseline algorithm maximum matching (MM), described in Wang et al. (1991), and the best bakeoff results. The *F-score*, *Roov and Riv* are summarized in Table 1, Table 2, and Table 3, respectively.

All the algorithms have quite similar recall for the in-vocabulary words (*Riv*), but their *Roov* vary greatly, which leads to the differences in F-score. In general both Algorithm 1 and Algorithm 2 improves OOV Recall significantly, compared with the baseline algorithm, maximum matching, which has barely any OOV recognition capacity. This confirms the effectiveness of the proposed phrase-based model in modeling morphological behaviors of characters. Moreover, Algorithm 2 works consistently better than Algorithm 1, which suggests the usefulness of its strategy of dealing with dependencies among phrase tokenizations.

Besides, the proposed method has the *linear* training and testing (when setting a maximum phrase length) time complexity, while the training complexity of CRF is the proportional to the feature numbers, which are often over millions. Even with current prototype, our method takes only minutes to build the model, in contrast with several hours that CRF segmenter needs to train the model for the same corpus on the same machine.

Admittedly, our model still underperforms the best systems in the bakeoff. This may be resulted from that 1) our system is still a prototype that ignores many minor issues and lack optimization and 2) as a generative model, our model may suffer more from the data sparseness problem, compared with discriminative models, such as CRF.

As mentioned earlier, the OOV recognition is the dominant factor that influences the overall accuracy. Different from the mechanism of tokenization combination in our approach, state-of-art systems such as those based on MaxEnt or CRF, achieve OOV recognition basically in the same way as in-dictionary word recognition. The segmentation is modeled as assigning labels to characters. And the probability of the label assignment for a character token is mostly determined by its features, which are usually local contexts in the form of character co-occurrences.

There are many other OOV recognition methods proposed in literature before the rise of machine learning in the field. For example, the Sproat et al. (1996) system can successfully recognize OOVs of strong patterns, such as Chinese personal names, transliterations, using finite-state techniques. Another typical example is Ma and Chen (2003), which proposed context free grammar like rules together with a recursive bottom-up merge algorithm that merges possible morphemes after an initial segmentation using maximum matching. It would be fairer to compare the OOV recognition performance of our approach with these methods, rather than maximum matching. But most earlier works are not evaluated on standard bake-off corpora and the implementations are not openly available, so it is difficult to make direct comparisons.

F-score	As	CityU	MSR	PKU
Best Bakeoff	0.952	0.943	0.964	0.950
Algorithm 2	0.919	0.911	0.946	0.912
Algorithm 1	0.897	0.888	0.922	0.890
MM	0.882	0.833	0.933	0.869

Table 1. The F-score over the bakeoff-2 data.

Roov	AS	CityU	MSR	PKU
Best Bakeoff	0.696	0.698	0.717	0.636
Algorithm 2	0.440	0.489	0.429	0.434
Algorithm 1	0.329	0.367	0.411	0.416
MM	0.004	0.000	0.000	0.059

Table 2. The Roov over the bakeoff-2 data.

Riv	AS	CityU	MSR	PKU
Best Bakeoff	0.963	0.961	0.968	0.972
Algorithm 2	0.961	0.961	0.970	0.951
Algorithm 1	0.955	0.940	0.950	0.940
MM	0.950	0.952	0.981	0.956

Table 3. The Riv over the bakeoff-2 data.

5 Conclusion

In this paper, we have presented the phrase-based tokenization for adaptive word segmentation. The proposed model is efficient in both training and decoding, which is desirable for fast model re-construction. It generalizes the traditional tokenization model by considering the phrase instead of the word as the segmentation hypothesis unit, which is capable of describing "morphemes in the context" and improves the OOV recognition performance significantly. Our approach decomposes sentence tokenization into phrase tokenizations. The final tokenization of the sentence is determined by finding the best combination of the tokenizations of phrases that cover the whole sentence. The tokenization hypotheses of a sentence are represented by a weighed directed acyclic graph called phrase tokenization lattice. Using this formalism, the sentence tokenization problem becomes a shortest path search problem on the graph.

In our model, one only needs to estimate the phrase tokenization probabilities in order to segment new sentences. The training is thus a linear time phrase extraction and maximum likelihood estimation procedure. We adopted a Viterbi-style dynamic programming algorithm to segment unseen sentences using the lattice. We also proposed a method called backward dependency match to model the dependencies of adjacent phrases to overcome the limitations of the assumption that tokenizations of neighboring phrases is independent. The experiment showed the effectiveness of the proposed phrase-based model in recognizing out-of-vocabulary words and its superior overall performance compared with the traditional tokenization model. It has both the efficiency of the tokenization model and the high performance of the character classification model.

One possible extension of the proposed model is to apply re-ranking techniques (Collins and Koo, 2005) to the k-best list generated by Algorithm 2. A second improvement would be to combine our model with other models in a log linear way as in Jiang et al. (2008). Since phrase-based tokenization is a model that can be accompanied by different training algorithms, it is also interesting to see whether discriminative training can lead to better performance.

Acknowledgments

The research leading to these results has received funding from the European Commission's 7th Framework Program under grant agreement n° 238405 (CLARA).

References

Adam Berger, Stephen Della Pietra, and Vincent Della Pietra. 1992. A Maximum Entropy Approach to Natural Language Processing. 1996. *Computational Linguistics*, 22(1): 39-71

Michael Collins and Terry Koo. 2005. Discriminative Reranking for Natural Language Parsing. *Computational Linguistics*, 31(1):25-69.

Thomas Emerson. 2005. The second international Chinese word segmentation bakeoff. In *Proceedings of Forth SIGHAN Workshop on Chinese Language Processing*. Jeju Island, Korea.

Jin Guo. 1997. Critical tokenization and its properties. *Computational Linguistics*, 23(4): 569-596

Qinan Hu, Haihua Pan, and Chunyu Kit. 2004. An example-based study on Chinese word segmentation using critical fragments. In *Proceedings of IJCNLP-2004*. Hainan Island, China

Changning Huang and Hai Zhao. 2007. Chinese Word Segmentation: a Decade Review. *Journal of Chinese Information Processing*, 21(3): 8-20

Chu-Ren Huang, Petr Simon, Shu-Kai Hsieh, and Laurent Prévot. Rethinking Chinese word segmentation: tokenization, character classification, or wordbreak identification. In *Proceedings of ACL-2007*. Prague, Czech

Liang Huang. 2008. Advanced dynamic programming in semiring and hypergraph frameworks. *In Proceedings of COLING 2008*. Manchester, UK.

Liang Huang and David Chiang. 2005. Better k-best parsing. In *Proceedings of the Ninth International Workshop on Parsing Technology*. Vancouver, Canada

Wenbin Jiang, Liang Huang, Qun Liu, Yajuan Lu. 2008. A Cascaded Linear Model for Joint Chinese Word Segmentation and Part-of-Speech Tagging. In *Proceedings of ACL 2008: HLT*. Columbus, USA

John Lafferty, Andrew McCallum, and Fernando Pereira. 2001. Conditional random fields: Probabilistic models for segmenting and labeling sequence data. In *Proceedings of ICML 2001*. Williamstown, MA, USA

Gina-Anne Levow. 2006. The third international Chinese language processing bakeoff: Word segmentation and named entity recognition. In *Proceedings of the Fifth SIGHAN Workshop on Chinese Language Processing*. Sydney, Australia

Nanyuan Liang. 1986. On computer automatic word segmentation of written Chinese. *Journal of Chinese Information Processing*, 1(1).

Wei-Yun Ma and Keh-Jiann Chen. 2003. A bottom-up merging algorithm for Chinese unknown word extraction. In *Proceedings of the second SIGHAN workshop on Chinese language processing*. Sapporo, Japan

Yan Ma. 1996. The study and realization of an evaluation-based automatic segmentation system. In Changning Huang and Ying Xia, editors, *Essays in Language Information Processing*. Tsinghua University Press, Beijing, China.

Mehryar Mohri. 2002. Semiring frameworks and algorithms for shortest-distance problems. *Journal of Automata, Languages and Combinatorics*, 7(3):321–350.

Fuchun Peng, Fangfang Feng, and Andrew McCallum. 2004. Chinese segmentation and new word detection using conditional random fields. In *Proceedings of COLING*. Stroudsburg, PA, USA.

Richard Sproat, Chilin Shih, William Gale, and Nancy Chang. 1996. A stochastic finite-state word-segmentation algorithm for Chinese. *Computational Linguistics*, 22(3):377-404.

Anand Venkataraman. 2001. A Statistical Model for Word Discovery in Transcribed Speech. *Computational Linguistics*, 27(3): 351-372

Andrew Viterbi (1967). Error bounds for convolutional codes and an asymptotically optimum decoding algorithm. *IEEE Transactions on Information Theory*, 13 (2): 260–269.

Xiaolong Wang, Kaizhu Wang, and Xiaohua Bai. 1991. Separating syllables and characters into words in natural language understanding. *Journal of Chinese Information Processing,* 5(3):48-58.

Nianwen Xue. 2003. Chinese Word Segmentation as Characater Tagging. *Computational Linguistics and Chinese Language Processing*, 8(1): 29-48

Hongmei Zhao and Qun Liu. 2010. The CIPS-SIGHAN CLP 2010 Chinese Word Segmentation Bakeoff. In *Proceedings of the First CPS-SIGHAN Joint Conference on Chinese Language Processing*. Beijing, China.

A Regularized Compression Method To Unsupervised Word Segmentation

Ruey-Cheng Chen, **Chiung-Min Tsai** and **Jieh Hsiang**
National Taiwan University
1 Roosevelt Rd. Sec. 4
Taipei 106, Taiwan
rueycheng@turing.csie.ntu.edu.tw
cmtsai@mail.lis.ntu.edu.tw
jhsiang@ntu.edu.tw

Abstract

Languages are constantly evolving through their users due to the need to communicate more efficiently. Under this hypothesis, we formulate unsupervised word segmentation as a regularized compression process. We reduce this process to an optimization problem, and propose a greedy inclusion solution. Preliminary test results on the Bernstein-Ratner corpus and Bakeoff-2005 show that the our method is comparable to the state-of-the-art in terms of effectiveness and efficiency.

1 Introduction

Unsupervised word segmentation has been a popular research subject due to its close connection to language acquisition. It has attracted researchers from different communities, including linguistics, cognitive science, and machine learning, to investigate how human beings develop and harness their languages, and, more importantly, how knowledge is acquired.

In this paper we propose a new formulation to the unsupervised word segmentation problem. Our idea is based on the observation that language evolves because of the need to reduce communication efforts. For instance, new terminologies, abbreviations, and slang that carry complex semantics which cannot be efficiently expressed in the original languages are invented so that concepts can be conveyed. Such an evolution, we hypothesize, is limited to the extent where the evolved vocabulary exhibits similar complexity as the original one, in light of reducing the extra cost to pick up the new language. This process is realized as an optimization problem called *regularized compression*, which gets this name from its analogy to text compression.

The rest of the paper is organized as follows. We briefly summarize related work on unsupervised word segmentation in Section 2. In Section 3, we introduce the proposed formulation. The iterative algorithm and other technical details for solving the optimization problem are covered in Section 4. In Section 5, we describe the evaluation procedure and discuss the experimental results. Finally, we present concluding remarks in Section 6.

2 Related Work

The past few years have seen many nonparametric Bayesian methods developed to model natural languages. Many such applications were applied to word segmentation and have collectively reshaped the entire research field. Two most notable examples are hierarchical Bayesian models and the minimum description length principle. Our method fits in the latter category since we use this principle to optimize model parameters.

Hierarchical Bayesian methods were first introduced to complement conventional probabilistic methods to facilitate context-aware word generation. Goldwater et al. (2006) used hierarchical Dirichlet processes (HDP) to induce contextual word models. Their approach was a significant improvement over conventional probabilistic methods, and has inspired further explorations into more advanced hierarchical modeling techniques. Such examples include the nested Pitman-Yor process (Mochihashi et al., 2009), a sophisticated installment for hierarchical modeling at both word and character levels, and adaptor grammars (Johnson and Goldwater, 2009), a framework that aligns HDP to probabilistic context-free grammars.

The minimum description length (MDL) principle, originally developed in the context of information theory, was adopted in Bayesian statistics as a principled model selection method (Rissanen, 1978). Its connection to lexical acquisition was first uncovered in behavioral studies, and early applications focused mostly on applying MDL to induce word segmentation that results in compact lexicons (Kit and Wilks, 1999; Yu, 2000; Argamon et al., 2004). More recent approaches (Zhikov et al., 2010; Hewlett and Cohen, 2011) used MDL in combination with existing algorithms, such as branching entropy (Tanaka-Ishii, 2005; Jin and Ishii, 2006) and bootstrap voting experts (Hewlett and Cohen, 2009), to determine the best segmentation parameters. On various benchmarks, MDL-powered algorithms have achieved state-of-the-art performance, sometimes even surpassing that of the most sophisticated hierarchical modeling methods.

3 Regularized Compression

3.1 Preliminaries

Consider that the unsegmented text consists of K utterances and totally of N characters. We denote the text as a sequence of characters $\mathbf{c} = \langle c_1, \ldots, c_N \rangle$, as if conceptually concatenating all the K utterances into one string. The positions of all the utterance boundaries in $\mathbf{c}$ are represented as a set $U = \{u_0 = 0, u_1, \ldots, u_K\}$. In other words, the k-th utterance ($k = 1, \ldots, K$) is stored as the subsequence $\langle c_{u_{k-1}+1}, \ldots, c_{u_k} \rangle$ in $\mathbf{c}$.

A segmented text is denoted as a sequence of words $\mathbf{w} = \langle w_1, w_2, \ldots, w_M \rangle$ for some $M < N$. It represents the same piece of text as $\mathbf{c}$ does. The word sequence $\mathbf{w}$ is said to *respect* the utterance boundaries U if any word in the sequence does not span over two utterances. Unique elements in a character or word sequence implicitly define an alphabet set (or lexicon). Hereafter, we denote such alphabet sets for $\mathbf{c}$ and $\mathbf{w}$ as $A_\mathbf{c}$ and $A_\mathbf{w}$, respectively.

3.2 Effects of Compression

Word segmentation results from compressing a sequence of characters. By compression, we mean to replace the occurrences for some k-characters subsequence $\langle c_1, c_2, \ldots, c_k \rangle$ in the text with those for a new string $w = c_1 c_2 \ldots c_k$ (word). This procedure can be generalized to include more subsequences to be replaced, each with a different length. The resulting sequence is a mixture of characters and words introduced during compression. For clarity, we use the term *token sequence* to refer to such a mixed sequence of characters or words.

Compression has a few effects to the token sequence: (i) it increases the total number of tokens, (ii) it expands the alphabet set to include newly produced tokens, (iii) it affects the entropy rate estimates. Note that, by seeing a token sequence as a series of outcomes drawn from some underlying stochastic process, we can estimate the entropy rate empirically.

Items (i) and (ii) are natural consequences of compression. The effort to describe the same piece of information gets reduced at the expense of expanding the vocabulary, and sometimes even changing the usage. A real-life example for this is that language users invent new terminologies for efficiently conveying complex information. Item (iii) describes something more subtle. Observe that, when some n occurrences of a k-character subsequence $\langle c_1, c_2, \ldots, c_k \rangle$ get compressed, each character c_i loses n occurrences, and totally nk occurrences move away from the subsequence; as a result, the newly created word w receives n occurrences. It is clear that compression has this side effect of redistributing probability masses among the observations (i.e., characters), thereby causing deviation to entropy rate estimates.

3.3 Formulation

The choice of subsequences to be compressed is essential in the aforementioned process. We hypothesize that a good choice has the following two properties: (i) higher frequency, and (ii) low deviation in entropy rate.

We motivate these two properties as follows. First, high frequency subsequences are favorable here since they are more likely to be character-level collocations; compressing these subsequences results in better compression rate. Second, deviation in entropy rate is reflected in vocabulary complexity, and we believe that it directly translates to efforts that language users pay to adapt to the new language. In this case, there seems no reason to believe that either increasing or decreasing vocabulary complexity is beneficial, since in two trivial "bad choices" that one can easily imagine, i.e., the text being fully segmented or unsegmented, the entropy rates reach both extremes.

Motivated by these observations, we expect that the best word segmentation (i) achieves some predefined compression rate, and (ii) minimizes deviation in entropy rate. This idea is realized as an optimization problem, called *regularized compression*. Conceptually, this problem is defined as:

$$\begin{array}{ll} \text{minimize} & \mathrm{DV}(\mathbf{c}, \mathbf{w}) \\ \text{subject to} & \mathbf{w} \text{ respects } U \\ & \left|\frac{|\mathbf{w}|}{|\mathbf{c}|} - \rho\right| \leq \epsilon \end{array} \tag{1}$$

where ρ denotes some expected compression ratio and ϵ denotes the tolerance. Note that $\mathrm{DV}(\mathbf{c}, \mathbf{w}) = |\tilde{H}(C) - \tilde{H}(W)|$ represents the deviation in entropy rate with respect to sequences $\mathbf{c}$ and $\mathbf{w}$. In this definition, $\tilde{H}(C)$ and $\tilde{H}(W)$ denote the empirical entropy rates for random variables $C \in A_{\mathbf{c}}$ and $W \in A_{\mathbf{w}}$, estimated on the corresponding sequences $\mathbf{c}$ and $\mathbf{w}$, respectively.

4 Iterative Algorithm

4.1 Ordered Ruleset

Acknowledging that exponentially many feasible word sequences need to be checked, we propose an alternative formulation in a restricted solution space. The idea is, instead of optimizing for segmentations, we search for *segmentation generators*, i.e., a set of functions that generate segmentations from the input. The generators we consider here is the *ordered rulesets*.

An ordered ruleset $R = \langle r_1, r_2, \ldots, r_k \rangle$ is a sequence of translation rules, each of which takes the following form:

$$w \rightarrow c_1 c_2 \ldots c_n,$$

where the right-hand side ($c_1 c_2 \ldots c_n$) denotes the n-token subsequence to be replaced, and the left-hand side (w) denotes the new token to be introduced. Applying a translation rule r to a token sequence has an effect of replacing all the occurrences for subsequence $c_1 c_2 \ldots c_n$ with those for token w.

Applying an ordered ruleset R to a token sequence is equivalent to iteratively applying the translation rules $r_1, r_2, \ldots, r_k$ in strict order. Specifically, consider that the initial token sequence is denoted as $\mathbf{c}^{(0)}$ and let the final result be denoted as $\mathbf{c}^{(k)}$. By iterative application, we mean to repeat the following step for $i = 1 \ldots k$:

> Apply rule r_i to $\mathbf{c}^{(i-1)}$ and save the result as $\mathbf{c}^{(i)}$.

4.2 Alternative Formulation

This notion of ordered rulesets allows one to explore the search space efficiently using a greedy inclusion algorithm. The idea is to maintain a globally best ruleset B that covers the best translation rules we have discovered so far, and then iteratively expand B by discovering new best rule and adding it to ruleset. The procedure repeats several times until the compression rate reaches some predefined ratio ρ. In each iteration, the best translation rule is determined by solving a modified version of Equation (1), which is written as follows:

$$\begin{array}{ll} \text{(In iteration } i\text{)} & \\ \text{minimize} & \alpha\frac{|\mathbf{c}^{(i)}|}{|\mathbf{c}^{(i-1)}|} + \mathrm{DV}(\mathbf{c}^{(i-1)}, \mathbf{c}^{(i)}) \\ \text{subject to} & r \text{ is a rule} \\ & r(\mathbf{c}^{(i-1)}) = \mathbf{c}^{(i)} \\ & \mathbf{c}^{(i)} \text{ respects } U \end{array} \tag{2}$$

Note that the alternative formulation is largely a greedy version of Equation (1) except a few minor changes. First, the compression rate constraint becomes the termination condition in the greedy inclusion algorithm. Second, we add an extra term $|\mathbf{c}^{(i)}|/|\mathbf{c}^{(i-1)}|$ to the objective to encourage early inclusion of frequent collocations. The trade-off parameter α is introduced in Equation (2) to scalarize both terms in the objective.

A brief sketch of the algorithm is given in the following paragraphs.

1. Let B be an empty ordered ruleset, and let $\mathbf{c}^{(0)}$ be the original sequence of tokens.

2. Repeat the following steps for each $i \in \mathcal{N}$, starting from $i = 1$, until the compression rate reaches some predefined threshold.
   (a) Find a rule r that maximizes Equation (2)
   (b) Apply the rule r to form a new sequence $\mathbf{c}^{(i)}$ from $\mathbf{c}^{(i-1)}$.
   (c) Add r to the end of B.
3. Output B and the final sequence.

4.3 Implementation

Additional care needs to be taken in implementing Steps 2a and 2b. The simplest way to collect n-gram counts for computing the objective in Equation (2) is to run multiple scans over the entire sequence. Our experience suggests that using an indexing structure that keeps track of token positions can be more efficient. This is especially important when updating the affected n-gram counts in each iteration. Since replacing one occurrence for any subsequence affects only its surrounding n-grams, the total number of such affected n-gram occurrences in one iteration is linear in the number of occurrences for the replaced subsequence. Using an indexing structure in this case has the advantage to reduce seek time. Note that, however, the overall running time remains in the same complexity class regardless of the deployment of an indexing structure. The time complexity for this algorithm is $O(TN)$, where T is the number of iterations and N is the length of the input sequence.

Although it is theoretically appealing to create an n-gram search algorithm, in this preliminary study we used a simple bigram-based implementation for efficiency. We considered only bigrams in creating translation rules, expecting that the discovered bigrams can grow into trigrams or higher-order n-grams in the subsequent iterations. To allow unmerged tokens (i.e., characters that was supposed to be in one n-gram but eventually left out due to bigram implementation) being merged into the discovered bigram, we also required that that one of the two participating tokens at the right-hand side of any translation rule has to be an unmerged token. This has a side effect to exclude generation of collocation-based words[1]. It can be an issue in certain standards; on the test corpora we used, this kind of problems is not obvious.

Another constraint that we added to the implementation is to limit the choice of bigrams to those has more frequency counts. Generally, the number of occurrence for any candidate bigram being considered in the search space has to be greater or equal to some predefined threshold. In practice, we found little difference in performance for specifying any integer between 3 and 7 as the threshold; in this paper, we stick to 3.

5 Evaluation

5.1 Setup

We conducted a series of experiments to investigate the effectiveness of the proposed segmentation method under different language settings and segmentation standards. In the first and the second experiments, we focus on drawing comparison between our method and state-of-the-art approaches. The third experiment focuses on the influence of data size to segmentation accuracy.

Segmentation performance is assessed using standard metrics, such as precision, recall, and F-measure. Generally, these measures are reported only at word level; in some cases where further analysis is called for, we report boundary-level and type-level measures as well. We used the evaluation script in the official HDP package to calculate these numbers.

The reference methods we considered in the comparative study include the following:

- Hierarchical Dirichlet process, denoted as HDP (Goldwater et al., 2009);
- Nested Pitman-Yor process, denoted as NPY (Mochihashi et al., 2009);
- Adaptor grammars, denoted as AG (Johnson and Goldwater, 2009);
- Branching entropy + MDL, denoted as Ent-MDL (Zhikov et al., 2010);
- Bootstrap voting experts + MDL, denoted as BVE-MDL (Hewlett and Cohen, 2011);
- Description length gain, denoted as DLG (Zhao and Kit, 2008).

[1]Fictional examples include "homework" or "cellphone".

The proposed method is denoted as RC; it is also denoted as RC-MDL in a few cases where MDL is used for parameter estimation.

5.2 Parameter Estimation

There are two free parameters α and ρ in our model. The parameter α specifies the degree to which we favors high-frequency collocations when solving Equation (2). Experimentation suggests that α can be sensitive when set too low[2]. Practically, we recommend optimizing α based on grid search on development data, or the MDL principle. The formula for calculating description length is not shown here; see Zhikov et al. (2010), Hewlett and Cohen (2011), and Rissanen (1978) for details.

The expected compression rate ρ determines when to stop the segmentor. It is related to the expected word length: When the compression rate $|\mathbf{c}|/|\mathbf{w}|$ reaches ρ and the segmentor is about to stop, $1/\rho$ is the average word length in the segmentation. In this sense, it seems ρ is somehow connected to the language of concern. We expect that optimal values learned on one data set may thus generalize on the other sets of the same language. Throughout the experiments, we estimated this value based on development data.

5.3 Evaluation on Bernstein-Ratner Corpus

We conducted the first experiment on the Bernstein-Ratner corpus (Bernstein-Ratner, 1987), a standard benchmark for English phonetic segmentation. We used the version derived by Michael Brent, which is made available in the CHILDES database (Brent and Cartwright, 1996; MacWhinney and Snow, 1990). The corpus comprises 9,790 utterances, which amount to 95,809 words in total. Its relatively small size allows experimentation with the most computational-intensive Bayesian models.

Parameter estimation for the proposed method has been a challenge due to the lack of appropriate development data. We first obtained a rough estimate for the compression rate ρ via human inspection into the first 10 lines of the corpus (these 10 lines were later excluded in evaluation) and used that estimate to set up the termination condition. Since the first 10 lines are too small to reveal any useful segmentation cues other than the word/token ration of interest, we considered this setting ("almost unsupervised") a reasonable compromise. In this experiment, ρ is set to 0.37; the trade-off parameter α is set to 8.3, optimized using MDL principle in a two-pass grid search (the first pass over $\{1, 2, \ldots, 20\}$ and the second over $\{8.0, 8.1, \ldots, 10.0\}$).

[2]Informally speaking, when $\alpha < \tilde{H}(\mathbf{c})$. The analysis is not covered in this preliminary study.

	P	R	F	Time
HDP	0.752	0.696	0.723	–
NPY, bigram	0.748	0.767	0.757	17 min.
AG	–	–	**0.890**	–
Ent-MDL	0.763	0.745	0.754	2.6 sec.
BVE-MDL	**0.793**	0.734	0.762	2.6 sec.
RC-MDL	0.771	**0.819**	0.794	0.9 sec.

Table 2: Performance evaluation on the Bernstein-Ratner corpus. The reported values for each method indicate word precision, recall, F-measure and running time, respectively. The boldface value for each column indicates the top performer under the corresponding metric.

A detailed performance result for the proposed method is described in Table 1. A reference run for HDP is included for comparison. The proposed method achieved satisfactory result at word and boundary levels. Nevertheless, low type-level numbers (in contrast to those for HDP) together with high boundary recall suggested that we might have experienced over-segmentation.

Table 2 covers the same result with less details in order to compare with other reference methods. All the reported measures for reference methods are directly taken from the literature. The result shows that AG achieved the best performance in F-measure (other metrics are not reported), surpassing all the other methods by a large margin (10 percent). Among the other methods, our method paired with MDL achieved comparable performance as the others in precision; it does slightly better than the others in recall (5 percent) and F-measure (2.5 percent). Furthermore, our algorithm also seems to be competitive in terms of computational efficiency. On this benchmark it demanded only minimal memory low as 4MB and finished the segmentation run in 0.9 second, even less than the reported running time for both MDL-based algorithms.

	P	R	F	BP	BR	BF	TP	TR	TF
HDP, Bernstein-Ratner	0.75	0.70	0.72	0.90	0.81	0.85	0.64	0.55	0.59
RC-MDL, Bernstein-Ratner	0.77	0.82	0.79	0.85	0.92	0.89	0.57	0.48	0.50
RC, CityU training	0.75	0.79	0.77	0.89	0.93	0.91	0.63	0.35	0.45
RC, MSR training	0.73	0.82	0.77	0.86	0.96	0.91	0.70	0.26	0.38

Table 1: Performance evaluation for the proposed method across different test corpora. The first row indicates a reference HDP run (Goldwater et al., 2009); the other rows represent the proposed method tested on different test corpora. Columns indicates performance metrics, which correspond to precision, recall, and F-measure at word (P/R/F), boundary (BP/BR/BF), and type (TP/TR/TF) levels.

Corpus	Training (W/T)	Test (W/T)
AS	5.45M / 141K	122K / 19K
PKU	1.1M / 55K	104K / 13K
CityU	1.46M / 69K	41K / 9K
MSR	2.37M / 88K	107K / 13K

Table 3: A short summary about the subsets in the Bakeoff-2005 dataset. The size of each subset is given in number of words (W) and number of unique word types (T).

	CityU	MSR
RC, $r = 0.65$	0.770	0.774
DLG, ensemble	0.684	0.665
Ent-MDL, $n_{max} = 3$	**0.798**	**0.795**

Table 4: Performance evaluation on the common training subsets in the Bakeoff-2005 and Bakeoff-2006 datasets. The reported values are token F-measure. The boldface value in each column indicates the top performer for the corresponding set.

5.4 Evaluation on Bakeoff-2005 Corpus

The second benchmark that we adopted is the SIGHAN Bakeoff-2005 dataset (Emerson, 2005) for Chinese word segmentation. The corpus has four separates subsets prepared by different research groups; it is among the largest word segmentation benchmarks available. Table 3 briefly summarizes the statistics regarding this dataset.

We decided to compare our algorithm with description length gain (DLG), for that it seems to deliver best segmentation accuracy among other unsupervised approaches ever reported on this benchmark (Zhao and Kit, 2008). Since the reported values for DLG were obtained on another closed dataset Bakeoff-2006 (Levow, 2006), we followed a similar experimental setup as suggested in the literature (Mochihashi et al., 2009): We compared both methods only on the training sets for the common subsets CityU and MSR. Note that this experimental setup departed slightly from that of Mochihashi et al. in that all the comparisons were strictly made on the training sets. The approach is more straightforward than the suggested sampling-based method.

Other baseline methods that we considered include HDP, Ent-MDL, and BVE-MDL, for their representativeness in segmentation performance and ease of implementation. The HDP implementation we used is a modified version of the offical HDP package[3]; we patched the package to make it work with Unicode-encoded Chinese characters. For Ent-MDL and BVE-MDL, we used the software package[4] distributed by Hewlett and Cohen (2011). We estimated the parameters using the AS training set as the development data. We set α to 6 based on a grid search. The expected compression rate ρ that we learned from the development data is 0.65.

In Table 1, we give a detailed listing of various performance measures for the proposed method. Segmentation performance seems moderate at both word and boundary levels. Nevertheless, high type precision and low type recall on both CityU and MSR training corpora signaled that our algorithm failed to discover most word types. This issue, we suspect, was caused by exclusion of low-frequency candidate bigrams, as discussed in Section 4.3.

Table 4 summarizes the result for word segmentation conducted on the CityU and MSR subsets of Bakeoff-2005. Due to practical computational limits, we were not able to run HDP and BVE-MDL on any complete subset. The result shows that our

[3]http://homepages.inf.ed.ac.uk/sgwater/

[4]http://code.google.com/p/voting-experts

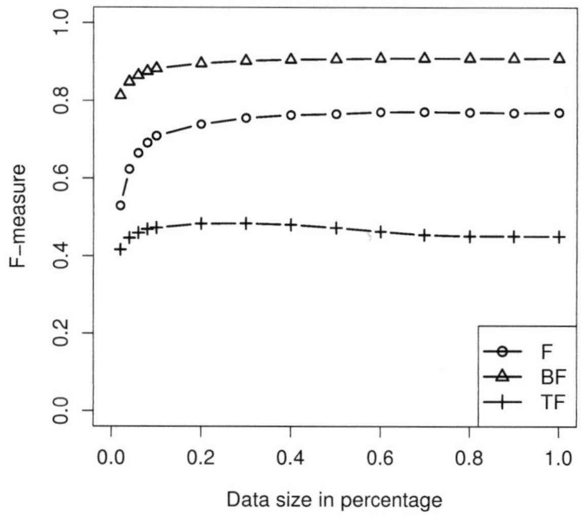

Figure 1: Performance evaluation for the proposed method on the CityU training set.

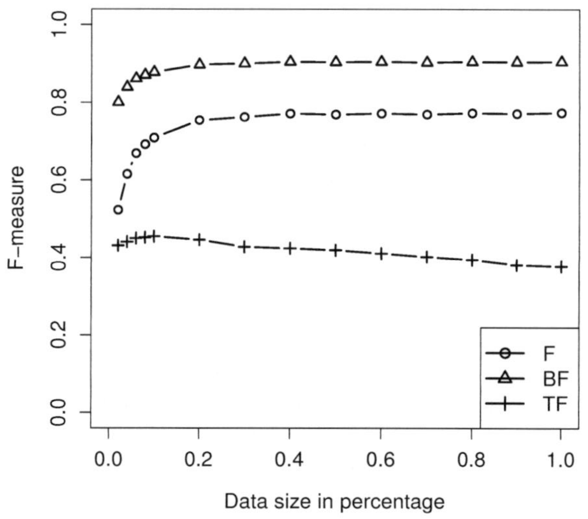

Figure 2: Performance evaluation for the proposed method on the MSR training set.

	CityU-1k	MSR-1k
RC, $r = 0.65$	0.505	0.492
HDP, 10 sample average	0.591	**0.623**
RC, $r = 0.65$/punc.	**0.599**	0.591

Table 5: Performance evaluation on two random samples from the common sets (CityU and MSR subsets) in the Bakeoff-2005 and Bakeoff-2006 datasets.

algorithm outperforms DLG by 8 to 10 percents in F-measure, while Ent-MDL still performs slightly better, achieving the top performance among all the experimental runs on both subsets.

To compare with HDP, we conducted another test run on top of a random sample of 1,000 lines from each subset. We chose 1,000 lines because HDP can easily consume more than 4GB of main memory on any larger sample. We adopted standard settings for HDP: $\alpha_0 = 3,000$, $\alpha_1 = 300$, and $p_b = 0.2$. In each trial run, we ran the Gibbs sampler for 20,000 iterations using simulated annealing (Goldwater et al., 2009). We obtained 10 samples from the Gibbs sampler and used the average performance in comparison. It took slightly more than 50 hours to collect one trial run on one subset.

The evaluation result is summarized in Table 5. We ran our algorithm to the desired compression ratio $r = 0.65$ on this small sample. The result shows that the performance of regularized compression is inferior to that of HDP by 9 to 13 percents in F-measure for both sets. To investigate why, we looked into the segmentation output. We observed that, in the regularized compression output, most of the punctuation marks were incorrectly aligned to their neighboring words, owing to the short of frequency counts in this small sample. The HDP, however, does not seem to suffer from this issue.

We devised a simple post-processing step, in which each punctuation mark was forced segmented from the surrounding text. Another outside test was conducted to see how well the algorithm works using heuristics derived from minimal domain knowledge. The additional run is denoted as RC/punc. The result is shown in Table 5. From the result, we found that the combined approach works slightly better than HDP in one corpus, but not in the other.

5.5 Effects of Data Size

We employed the third experiment to study the influence of corpora size to segmentation accuracy. Since the proposed method relies on empirical estimates for entropy rate to decide the word boundaries, we were interested in learning about how it responds to relatively low and high volume input.

This experiment was conducted on CityU and

MSR training sets. On each corpus, we took the first $k\%$ of data (in terms of utterances) and tested the proposed method against that subset; this test was repeated several times with different values for k. In this experiment, we chose the value for k from the set $\{2, 4, 6, 8, 10, 20, 30, \ldots, 90, 100\}$. The performance is evaluated using word, boundary, and type F-measures.

Figures 1 and 2 show the experiment results. Both figures revealed similar patterns for segmentation performance at different volume levels. Word F-measures for both corpora begin at roughly 0.52, climb up rapidly to 0.73 as the volume grows from 2% to 20%, and finally settle on some value around 0.77. Boundary F-measures for both corpora show a similar trend—a less steep increase before 20% from 0.80 to 0.89 followed by a plateau at around 0.93. Here, the result seems to suggest that estimating token entropy rate using less than 20% of data might be insufficient for this type of text corpora. Furthermore, since performance is saturated at such an early stage, it seems feasible to split the entire dataset into a number of folds (e.g., 5, in this case) and solve each fold individually in parallel. This technique may greatly enhance the run-time efficiency of the segmentor.

The patterns we observed for type F-measure tells another story. On both corpora, type F-measures do not seem to improve as data volume increases. On CityU corpora, type F-measure gradually increased from 0.42 to 0.48 and then slowly falling back to 0.45. On MSR corpora, type F-measure peaked at 0.45 when receiving 10% of data; after that it started decreasing, going all the way down to 0.37, even lower than the number 0.43 it received at the beginning. Our guess is that, at some early point (20%), the proposed method started to under-segment the text. We suspect that there is some deep connection between performance saturation and under-segmentation, since from the result they both begin at roughly the same level. Further investigation in this respect is needed to give out definitive explanations.

6 Concluding Remarks

Preliminary experimental results suggest that the regularized compression method, even only with partial evidence, seems as effective as the state-of-the-art methods in different language settings. When paired with MDL criteria, regularized compression is comparable to hierarchical Bayesian methods and MDL-based algorithms in terms of segmentation accuracy and computational efficiency. Furthermore, regularized compression is less memory-demanding than the other approaches; thus, it scales more easily to large corpora for carrying out certain tasks such as segmenting historical texts written in ancient languages, or preprocessing a large dataset for subsequent manual annotation.

We have identified a number of limitations of regular compression. First, the choice of candidate n-grams does not cover *hapax legomena*, i.e., words that occur only once in the corpus. At present, precluding these low-frequency n-grams seems to be a necessary compromise due to our limited understanding about the dynamics behind regular compression. Second, regularized compression does not work well with low volume data, since on smaller dataset the distribution of frequency counts is less precise. Third, the algorithm may stop identifying new word types at some point. We suspect that this is related to the choice of n-gram, since in our implementation no two existing "words" can be aggregated into one. These issues shall be addressed in our future work.

Acknowledgments

We thank the anonymous reviewers for their valuable comments. The research efforts described in this paper are supported under the National Taiwan University Digital Archives Project (Project No. NSC-98-2631-H-002-005), which is sponsored by National Science Council, Taiwan.

References

Shlomo Argamon, Navot Akiva, Amihood Amir, and Oren Kapah. 2004. Efficient unsupervised recursive word segmentation using minimum description length. In *Proceedings of the 20th international conference on Computational Linguistics*, COLING '04, Stroudsburg, PA, USA. Association for Computational Linguistics.

Nan Bernstein-Ratner. 1987. The phonology of parent child speech. *Children's language*, 6:159–174.

Michael R. Brent and Timothy A. Cartwright. 1996. Distributional regularity and phonotactic constraints are useful for segmentation. In *Cognition*, pages 93–125.

Thomas Emerson. 2005. The second international chinese word segmentation bakeoff. In *Proceedings of the Fourth SIGHAN Workshop on Chinese Language Processing*, volume 133. Jeju Island, Korea.

Sharon Goldwater, Thomas L. Griffiths, and Mark Johnson. 2006. Contextual dependencies in unsupervised word segmentation. In *Proceedings of the 21st International Conference on Computational Linguistics and the 44th annual meeting of the Association for Computational Linguistics*, ACL-44, pages 673–680, Stroudsburg, PA, USA. Association for Computational Linguistics.

Sharon Goldwater, Thomas L. Griffiths, and Mark Johnson. 2009. A bayesian framework for word segmentation: Exploring the effects of context. *Cognition*, 112(1):21–54, July.

Daniel Hewlett and Paul Cohen. 2009. Bootstrap voting experts. In *Proceedings of the 21st international jont conference on Artifical intelligence*, IJCAI'09, pages 1071–1076, San Francisco, CA, USA. Morgan Kaufmann Publishers Inc.

Daniel Hewlett and Paul Cohen. 2011. Fully unsupervised word segmentation with BVE and MDL. In *Proceedings of the 49th Annual Meeting of the Association for Computational Linguistics: Human Language Technologies: short papers - Volume 2*, HLT '11, pages 540–545, Stroudsburg, PA, USA. Association for Computational Linguistics.

Zhihui Jin and Kumiko T. Ishii. 2006. Unsupervised segmentation of chinese text by use of branching entropy. In *Proceedings of the COLING/ACL on Main conference poster sessions*, COLING-ACL '06, pages 428–435, Stroudsburg, PA, USA. Association for Computational Linguistics.

Mark Johnson and Sharon Goldwater. 2009. Improving nonparameteric bayesian inference: experiments on unsupervised word segmentation with adaptor grammars. In *Proceedings of Human Language Technologies: The 2009 Annual Conference of the North American Chapter of the Association for Computational Linguistics*, NAACL '09, pages 317–325, Stroudsburg, PA, USA. Association for Computational Linguistics.

Chunyu Kit and Yorick Wilks. 1999. Unsupervised learning of word boundary with description length gain. In *CoNLL-99*, pages 1–6, Bergen, Norway.

Gina-Anne Levow. 2006. The third international chinese language processing bakeoff: Word segmentation and named entity recognition. In *Proceedings of the Fifth SIGHAN Workshop on Chinese Language Processing*, volume 117. Sydney: July.

Brian MacWhinney and Catherine Snow. 1990. The child language data exchange system: an update. *Journal of child language*, 17(2):457–472, June.

Daichi Mochihashi, Takeshi Yamada, and Naonori Ueda. 2009. Bayesian unsupervised word segmentation with nested Pitman-Yor language modeling. In *Proceedings of the Joint Conference of the 47th Annual Meeting of the ACL and the 4th International Joint Conference on Natural Language Processing of the AFNLP: Volume 1 - Volume 1*, ACL '09, pages 100–108, Stroudsburg, PA, USA. Association for Computational Linguistics.

Jorma Rissanen. 1978. Modeling by shortest data description. *Automatica*, 14(5):465–471, September.

Kumiko Tanaka-Ishii. 2005. Entropy as an indicator of context boundaries: An experiment using a web search engine. In Robert Dale, Kam-Fai Wong, Jian Su, and Oi Kwong, editors, *Natural Language Processing IJCNLP 2005*, volume 3651 of *Lecture Notes in Computer Science*, chapter 9, pages 93–105. Springer Berlin / Heidelberg, Berlin, Heidelberg.

Hua Yu. 2000. Unsupervised word induction using MDL criterion. In *Proceedings of the International Symposium of Chinese Spoken Language Processing*, Beijin, China.

Hai Zhao and Chunyu Kit. 2008. An empirical comparison of goodness measures for unsupervised chinese word segmentation with a unified framework. In *The Third International Joint Conference on Natural Language Processing (IJCNLP-2008)*.

Valentin Zhikov, Hiroya Takamura, and Manabu Okumura. 2010. An efficient algorithm for unsupervised word segmentation with branching entropy and MDL. In *Proceedings of the 2010 Conference on Empirical Methods in Natural Language Processing*, EMNLP '10, pages 832–842, Stroudsburg, PA, USA. Association for Computational Linguistics.

A rule-based approach to unknown word recognition in Arabic

Lynne Cahill
NLTG, University of Brighton
Lewes Rd, Brighton
BN2 4GJ, UK
L.Cahill@brighton.ac.uk

Abstract

This paper describes a small experiment to test a rule-based approach to unknown word recognition in Arabic. The morphological complexity of Arabic presents its challenges to a variety of NLP applications, but it can also be viewed as an advantage, if we can tap into the complex linguistic knowledge associated with these complex forms. In particular, the derived forms of verbs can be analysed and an educated guess at the likely meaning of a derived form can be predicted, based on the meaning of a known form and the relationship between the known form and the unknown one. The performance of the approach is tested on the NEMLAR Written Arabic Corpus.

1 Introduction

The Semitic languages, especially Arabic, are linguistically interesting for a number of reasons, and are attracting more and more attention for both linguistic and socio-political reasons. One of the aspects of Arabic that makes it particularly interesting to linguists, namely the morphological complexity, is at once both appealing and the source of potential practical problems. It is appealing to linguists, for whom it offers interesting challenges in their descriptive frameworks, but for builders of NLP applications, it represents a significant challenge. In this paper, we are particularly interested in the derivational aspects of the morphology, whereby verb stems are derived from triliteral roots in well defined formal ways, and with varying degrees of regularity in the meanings of those derived forms.

Another aspect of the Arabic language that makes it both interesting and challenging is the fact that it is not actually a single language. There are many varieties of Arabic, with rather different status. Classical Arabic (CA) is the language of the Koran, and the historical ancestor of the other varieties. Modern Standard Arabic (MSA) is the modern version of CA and is, broadly speaking, the universal (i.e. not regional) standard variety of Arabic. Until recently, CA and MSA were the only varieties that were written – other, regional, varieties were only spoken. The situation is rapidly changing, with electronic communication increasingly involving written versions of the regional varieties. Even in traditional written forms, such as news reports, the vocabulary used in different geographical regions is different. For example, Khoja (2001) found that the percentage of out of vocabulary items in news reports from Egypt and Qatar was around double that found in Saudi news reports, Saudi Arabic being much closer to MSA than the other two regional varieties. Ways in which the present approach may assist in this problem will be discussed later.

The approach we describe here depends on a hierarchically organised lexicon, based on the DATR lexical representation language (Evans and Gazdar, 1996). The PolyLex lexical framework (Cahill and Gazdar, 1999) was developed originally with languages like English, German and Dutch in mind, but has been shown to lend itself to the description of Arabic templatic morphology (Cahill, 2007, 2010). The inheritance of information by default in this framework is fundamental to the approach we describe.

The problem to which we seek a solution is not one unique to Arabic. Any NLP system which wants to process naturally occurring text will always have to deal to some degree with the problem of unknown or out of vocabulary (OOV) items. Whether these items are neologisms, errors or names, they need to be handled in some way. Solutions to this particular problem are unlikely to have a large statistical impact on the success rates of the processing applications, but that does not mean that they are not worth finding. While it is undoubtedly the case that many applications will work perfectly well with a word recognition rate of, say, 95%, supported by statistical approaches which provide syntactic information, there are other applications for which full semantic interpretation is desirable, if not necessary. It is such applications that the current paper addresses. We are only addressing a part of the problem, as this approach does not help recognise names or errors.

The particular approach described in this paper is based on the observation that a native speaker who encounters a word they have not seen before may, if that word is related to others that they do know, be able to make an educated guess at not only the syntactic category, but also the meaning of that word. To a large degree, that guesswork involves the specific context that the word occurs in, but native speakers will also have more abstract structural knowledge about their language which allows them to make guesses about words on the basis of their internal structure. For example, if an English speaker knows the word "confuse" and hears the word "confuser", even though they have most likely never before come across the latter, they will be able to at least guess that it means "someone/thing that confuses". Of course, with derivation the meaning relationship is not always transparent. So a person encountering the word "decider" for the first time may be surprised to find that it does not mean "one who decides" but rather a deciding match/game etc.. Such issues and other limitations of this approach will be discussed later.

2 Previous approaches

There has been a lot of work on how to handle OOV items, largely based on statistical approaches. Some are language independent (see e.g. Attia et al (2010), Adler et al (2008)) while others focus on specific languages (see e.g. Habash and Rambow (2005, 2007) and Marsi et al (2005) on Arabic and Adler and Elhadad (2006) on Hebrew, another Semitic language with similar morphological structure). The work by Habash and Rambow, for example, employs a form of morphological expansion to handle OOV items, but only makes use of the inflectional morphology of Arabic, not the derivational morphology as in the current approach.

Other approaches to morphological analysis in Arabic include methods to deal with OOV items. For example, Beesley and Karttunen (2003), describe a two-level approach which includes a general method for guessing OOV words which could certainly apply to some degree to Arabic, but it would not be able to take into account the linguistic (specifically semantic) information which is at the heart of the present approach.

3 PolyLex/PolyOrth

The PolyLex project (Cahill and Gazdar, 1999) developed multilingual lexicons of the morphology and phonology of English, German and Dutch, implemented in the lexical representation language DATR (Evans and Gazdar, 1996) which allows for default inheritance. Therefore, aspects of these languages that were shared could be inherited by default by each language.

In addition to the aspects of inter- and intra-language default inheritance, the other aspect of the PolyLex framework which contributes to the unknown word processing proposed here is the use of phonological structures, specifically syllables, to define morphological structures and relationships. Thus, in PolyLex, the lexical entries consist of specifications of the phonological forms of the syllable constituents (onset, peak and coda). These can be determined by morpho-syntactic features. For example, the English word *man* has default values for the onset (/m/), peak (/æ/) and coda (/n/), but a further value for the peak in the plural (/ɛ/). This is represented in DATR as[1]:

```
<phn syl1 onset> == m
<phn syl1 peak> == {
<phn syl1 coda> == n
<phn syl1 peak plur> == E.
```

The PolyOrth project (Cahill et al. 2006) further developed the representation so that orthographic

[1] In the DATR code, the SAMPA machine readable alphabet (Wells, 1989) is used.

forms are derived by means of a combination of phoneme-grapheme mappings and spelling rules. Both types of information include phonological and morphological determinants, so that, for example, the default mapping for any particular phoneme will depend on both its phonological position (is it in the onset or coda?) and on its morphological position (is it in a stem or an affix?). Both types of information are defined by means of Finite State Transducers (FSTs)[2]. This framework has been implemented and tested on English, German and Dutch, and now extended to Arabic (Cahill, 2010). The Arabic lexicon allows for forms to be defined in Arabic script, Roman transliteration or phonological representation.

4 Arabic verbal morphology

The Arabic languages have around 280 million speakers. They belong to the Semitic language family, and share many linguistic features with other Semitic languages, such as Hebrew and Maltese. Much work in both theoretical and computational linguistics has focused on the so-called templatic morphology of the Semitic languages.

The key area of Arabic morphology addressed in this paper is the verbal derivation. Verbs in Arabic are typically based on a tri-literal root, consisting of three consonants. Inflectional variation involves interdigitating these consonants with vowels which indicate the tense, aspect and mood. In addition, the three consonants can be differently arranged (doubled, swapped etc.) to form distinct Forms (or measures, also known as binyanim[3], especially when applied to Hebrew). These are essentially derivations and form distinct verbs with different meanings. For example, the tri-literal root *k-t-b* has the core meaning "write". The forms *katabtu* and *aktubtu*, represent the active perfective and active imperfective first person singular forms of "write", namely, "I wrote" and "I write". The second Form or measure verb *k-tt-b* also has the inflectional variations, but has the meaning "cause to write", thus the two actual forms *kattabtu* and *akttabtu* have the meanings "I caused (someone) to write" and "I cause (someone) to write" respectively.

There are fifteen different Forms in CA, but fewer in the modern varieties. In MSA there are ten that are commonly found, although two more are found rarely. The regional varieties all make use of fewer. While some of the Forms have clear transparent meanings, others have far less clear or apparently random meaning relations.

The following descriptions of the meanings of the ten Forms is adapted from Scheindlin (2007):

I. The basic Form – all verbs have this form. May be transitive or intransitive.
II. Almost always transitive. If a verb exists in both Form I and II then I will often be intransitive and II transitive (*write* (I) → *cause to write* (II)). If I is transitive then II may be ditransitive. II may also involve an intensifying of the meaning on I, e.g. *kill* (I) → *massacre* (II).
III. May involve reciprocity, e.g. *follow* (I) → *alternate* (III).
IV. Like II, mostly transitive, and often matched with intransitive in I.
V. Often involves a reflexive element, e.g. *know* (I) → *teach* (II) → *learn* (V).
VI. Like III, often involves reciprocity, e.g. *fight* (I) → *fight each other* (VI).
VII. Mostly reflexive, resultative or passive. Roots that are transitive in I are intransitive in VII. E.g. *break* (I) → *be broken* (VII).
VIII. Often reflexive for verbs that are transitive in I, e.g. *divide* (I) → *part* (VIII).
IX. Very restricted in application, only applying to verbs indicating colours and defects, e.g. *turn yellow*.
X. Often associated with asking for something associated with the Form I verb, e.g. *pardon* (I) → *apologise (ask for pardon)* (X).

As is clear from these descriptions, the meaning relationships are not fully predictable, but they can give some hints as to the likely meaning of an unknown verb. As the framework relies on default inheritance, the assumption that any definitions may be overridden by more specific information means that even very approximate definitions are still valuable.

[2] The PolyOrth project was inspired by Herring (2006). However, while Herring uses one-stage FSTs, the PolyOrth project used two levels of FST, including a separate treatment of "post-lexical" spelling rules.
[3] We will use the term "Form", capitalised to avoid confusion with the more usual use of "form".

5 Arabic in syllable-based morphology

A small sample lexicon of Arabic in the PolyLex framework is presented in Cahill (2007). What makes this account different from most accounts of the morphology of the Semitic languages is that it requires no special apparatus to allow for the definition of so-called "templatic" morphology, but makes use of the same kind of equations as are required for ablaut and consonant devoicing, for example, that are found in English, German and Dutch.

5.1 The default, Form I root

The main part of the account addresses a single verb root, namely *k.t.b*, 'write', and generates all possible Form stems for perfective, imperfective and participle, active and passive. The approach is based on defining the leaves of syllable-structure trees, with the consonants of the triliteral stems occupying the onset and coda positions, and the vowels (syllable peaks) being defined according to the morphosyntactic specification, as in the example of *man* above. To illustrate this, the figure below shows the default structure for a triliteral root, with no vowels specified. The default structure is a disyllabic root, with the first consonant occupying the onset of the first syllable, the second consonant occupying the onset of the second syllable and the third consonant occupying the coda of the second syllable[4].

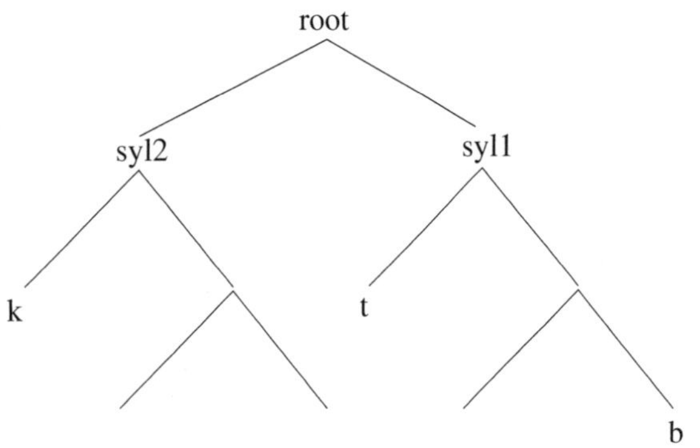

Figure 1: the structure of /katab/

[4] The syllable position is indicated by simple numbering. Syllables can be counted from either right of left. For languages which largely use suffixation, it makes more sense to count from the right, as for Arabic here.

5.2 The other Form stems

As described in Cahill (2007), the remaining nine forms have their default structure defined in similar terms. Figure 2 depicts the inheritance of forms from each other. This inheritance is for the syllable structure definitions, so the Form II structure is the same as the Form I structure except that the first coda has the value of the second root consonant, the same as the onset of the second syllable. The definitions are all incremental, so that each Form specification only supplies one or two pieces of information.

5.3 Meanings

The original lexicon was designed to demonstrate that the complex relationships between phonological, morphological and orthographic forms in Arabic could be captured in the PolyLex/PolyOrth architecture. There was no semantic information in the lexicons at all. For the present experiment, we have added very basic semantic information for the 100 verbs we have included. Most of these are Form I verbs, but there are some Form II, Form IV and Form V verbs. Where possible, we have represented the meanings of the verbs of Forms other than I in terms that can be generalised. For example, the verb *apologise* has the meaning expressed as ASK FOR PARDON[5].

The lexical hierarchy, in addition, defines a default meaning expression for each Form. For Form VIII, for example, this is:

```
<meaning> == ask for "<formI meaning>"
```

which says that the meaning is simply the string "ask for" followed by the meaning for Form I for the root[6].

5.4 The full lexicon

[5] For this small experiment, the exact representation of the meanings is not important. It is assumed that in a genuine application will have its representations which would be included in the lexicon, or for which a mapping can be defined.

[6] The quotes around the path <form1 meaning> indicate that it is to be evaluated at the original query node, i.e. the root node in DATR.

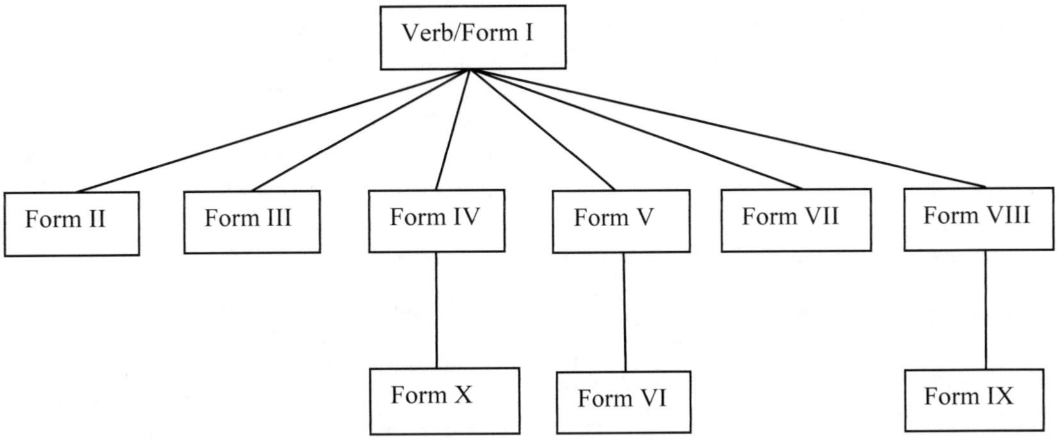

Figure 2: The inheritance of Forms

As stated above, the lexicon we are working from has only 100 verbs. There are no verb roots for which we have more than one Form. This is a very small number, but for each verb in the lexicon there are a theoretically possible further nine verbs which may be derived from the same root. The lexicon will recognise any theoretically possible verb from the roots it knows about, although it does not have semantic information explicitly provided for a large proportion of these verbs.

6 Using the lexicon for word recognition

The highly structured, hierarchical lexicons are not designed to be used as they are within NLP applications. The information in them is cached in a lookup table which can be used for either generation or comprehension, with entries which look like this:

كتب	k-t-b	katab	stem	p, a	k-t-b	I	write
كتتب	k-tt-b	kattab	stem	p, p	k-t-b	II	[cause to write]

The first column is the form in Arabic script, the second is the transliteration, the third is one possible full (vowelised) form, the fourth and fifth give the morphological analysis, the sixth is the triliteral root it is derived from, the seventh is the Form and the last is the translation. The first row, which has the Form I entry, has a translation which was provided explicitly in the lexicon but the second gets its meaning by default. This is indicated by the square brackets. In use in an application, these meanings would be used more cautiously, possibly in conjunction with other methods, especially making use of context.

The lookup table often provides more than one possible entry for a single form, especially when the form is unvowelised.

6.1 Testing

In order to test the approach, we tested the recognition of all verbs in the NEMLAR written corpus (Attiyya et al., 2005). The corpus provides versions with POS tagging, which enabled us to extract each verb. There were a total of just over 40,000 forms tagged as verbs, approximately 11,000 of them unique forms. Initial tests only took those forms which were tagged as having neither prefix nor suffix, a total of 1274 verb forms[7]. These included forms which were inflectionally distinct, and once these forms were collapsed, the total number of verb forms is 577. Of these, 32 occurred in our initial lexicon of 100 verbs.

These tests showed that of the remaining 545 unknown verbs, 84 could apparently be analysed as derived forms of one of our existing verbs. This

[7] The decision to use only those forms without prefix of suffix was simply made to make the testing process simpler and to ensure that the results were not skewed by the presence of consonants in prefixes or suffixes.

was determined by checking the main entries in an online Arabic dictionary and comparing the meanings given to those generated by the lexicon. This was a very promising figure, given the very small size of the lexicon.[8]

In the next testing phase we looked more closely at these forms. There are two ways in which the analyses may not be appropriate. The analysis might not be an appropriate (or at least not the most appropriate) one. This is not a major problem since we are dealing with a situation in which we frequently have multiple possible analyses for a word, so generating a number of possibilities from which an application must choose is exactly what is required. The second issue is the question of whether the meanings generated are useful. In order to check this we manually compared the generated meanings against the actual meanings for a sample of the verbs in question. We found that just over half of the verbs we checked had meanings which were at least clearly connected to the generated meaning. For example, the stem علّم (*teach*) is clearly related to the stem علم (*know*), and turns out to be the second Form ("cause to X") of the root for which *know* is the first Form.

6.2 Analysis of results

The verbs for which meanings were generated fit into three broad categories. First there are verbs for which the derived Form appears in dictionaries with the same meaning as that for Form I, possibly as one of its meanings. Thus, for example, the Form VIII verb *ktatab* had the meaning "wrote", the same as the Form I *katab*. There were 23 verbs in our set of 84 for which this was the case.

The second category consists of verbs for which the meaning is related in the way suggested by our earlier analysis. 22 of the verbs came into this category.[9]

Finally, the last category consists of verbs whose meaning is not related in the way suggested. This is the most problematic class, and unfortunately the largest in the small test set we are working with. However, in most, indeed nearly all, of these cases, the generated meaning was not wildly different from that in the dictionary. Closer inspection suggests that simply improving the meaning relations, and allowing more than one additional possible lexicon entry for some Forms would improve the performance significantly.

7 Discussion and conclusion

This paper has described a small experiment to test a novel rule-based approach to unknown word recognition in Arabic. Although testing is at an early stage, the initial results are promising.

The experiment described is intended to address a small part of the overall problem of unknown words. In some respects it can be viewed as more of a technique for extending an existing lexicon than for dealing with OOV items at runtime. However, it would be possible to enable an application to have access to the default lexical information at runtime, to allow this.

Another area in which the above technique may prove particularly useful is in the processing of regional varieties of Arabic. As stated above, Khoja (2001) found that even texts apparently written in MSA were twice as likely to have unknown words in texts from Egypt and Qatar than from Saudi Arabia. This suggests some variation in the vocabulary, most likely involving "leakage" of vocabulary items from Egyptian and Qatari Arabic into the MSA used by those speakers. As the morphological patterns of derived verbs are different in the different regional varieties, taking these patterns into account will provide further possible interpretations. The PolyLex structure allows the definition of similarities and differences between the lexicons of languages and dialects that are closely related.

7.1 Limitations and future work

The experiment described here is a very small scale one, and the lexicon is extremely small. The representation of meaning is also extremely simplified. It is possible that the approach described simply could not be scaled up to a size useful for an application. However, there is a range of ways

[8] There were some difficulties with transliteration which mean that these figures may not be fully accurate.

[9] This is clearly a case of subjective judgement, and from a non-native speaker these judgements may not be accurate.

of representing meaning, including linking to an external ontology, which could also be implemented in the lexicon described.

The next phase of work is to fully evaluate the results of the initial tests, followed by further more extensive testing. It is envisaged that an iterated cycle of testing and extension of the lexicon could lead to a lexicon large enough to be useful and robust enough to handle significant (if still small) numbers of OOV items.

Subsequently, and further down the line, development of a lexicon (or lexicons) for the vocabulary of regional varieties, linked to the MSA lexicon in the PolyLex framework will help to exploit the similarities. That is, the lexicon for, say, Egyptian Arabic assumes that, by default, words are the same as in MSA, with only those words (morphemes, phonemes etc.) which differ requiring specification.

Acknowledgements

The work described here was partly supported by the ESRC (Economic and Social Research Council, UK) as part of the project: **RES-000-22-3868** *Orthography, phonology and morphology in the Arabic lexicon*. We are grateful to the anonymous reviewers for their helpful comments.

References

Adler, Meni and Michael Elhadad. () An Unsupervised Morpheme-Based HMM for Hebrew Morphological Disambiguation. *COLING-ACL 2006*, pp. 665-672.

Adler, Meni, Yoav Goldberg, David Gabay and Michael Elhadad. (2008) Unsupervised Lexicon-Based Resolution of Unknown Words for Full Morphological Analysis. *ACL-08 : HLT*, pp. 728-36.

Atiyya, Muhammed, Khalid Choukri and Mustafa Yaseen. (2005) *The NMELAR Written Corpus* ELDA.

Attia, Mohammed, Jennifer Foster, Deirdre Hogan, Joseph Le Roux, Lamia Tounsi and Josef van Genabith. (2010) Handling Unknown Words in Statistical Latent-Variable Parsing Models for Arabic, English and French. *NAACL HLT Workshop on Statistical Parsing of Morphologically Rich Languages*. pp. 67-75.

Beesley, Kenneth and Lauri Karttunen. (2003) *Finite State Morphology* Chicago : CSLI.

Cahill, Lynne. (2010) A Syllable-based Approach to verbal Morphology in Arabic. *Workshop on Semitic Languages, LREC2010*, Malta, 2010.

Cahill, Lynne. (2007) A Syllable-based Account of Arabic Morphology. In Abdelhadi Soudi, Antal van der Bosch and Günther Neumann (eds.) *Arabic Computational Morphology* Dordrecht : Springer. pp. 45-66.

Cahill, Lynne, Jon Herring and Carole Tiberius, "PolyOrth: Adding Orthography to a Phonological Inheritance Lexicon", *Fifth International Workshop on Writing Systems*, Nijmegen, Netherlands, October 2006 (available at http://www.nltg.brighton.ac.uk/projects/polyorth).

Cahill, Lynne and Gazdar, Gerald. (1999) The PolyLex architecture : multilingual lexicons for related languages. *Traitement Automatique des Langues*, 40 :2, pp. 5-23.

Evans, Roger and Gazdar, Gerald. (1996) DATR : a language for lexical knowledge representation. *Computational Linguistics*, 22 :2, pp. 167-216.

Habash, Nizar and Owen Rambow. (2007) Arabic Diacritization through Full Morphological Tagging. *NAACL HLT 2007*pp. 53-56.

Habash, Nizar and Owen Rambow. (2005) Arabic Tokenization, Part-of-Speech Tagging and Morphological Disambiguation in One Fell Swoop. *ACL 2005*, pp. 573-80.

Herring, J. (2006) *Orthography and the lexicon*, PhD dissertation, University of Brighton.

Khoja, Shereen. (2001) APT: Arabic Part-of-speech Tagger. *Proceedings of the Student Workshop at the Second Meeting of the North American Chapter of the Association for Computational Linguistics (NAACL2001).*

Marsi, Erwin, Antal van den Bosch and Abdelhadi Soudi. (2005) Memory-based morphological analysis, generation and part-of-speech tagging of Arabic. *ACL Workshop on Computational Approaches to Semitic Languages*. pp. 1-8.

Scheindlin, Raymond P. (2007) *501 Arabic verbs* Haupage: Barron.

Wells, John. (1989) Computer-coded phonemic notation of individual languages of the European Community. *Journal of the International Phonetic Association*, 19 :1, pp. 31-54.

Bounded copying is subsequential: Implications for metathesis and reduplication*

Jane Chandlee
Linguistics and Cognitive Science
University of Delaware
Newark, DE
janemc@udel.edu

Jeffrey Heinz
Linguistics and Cognitive Science
University of Delaware
Newark, DE
heinz@udel.edu

Abstract

This paper first defines the conditions under which copying and deletion processes are subsequential: specifically this is the case when the process is bounded in the right ways. Then, if we analyze metathesis as the composition of copying and deletion, it can be shown that the set of attested metathesis patterns fall into the subsequential or reverse subsequential classes. The implications of bounded copying are extended to partial reduplication, which is also shown to be either subsequential or reverse subsequential.

1 Introduction

This paper presents a computational analysis of copying and deletion in metathesis and partial reduplication and establishes the necessary conditions for such patterns to be subsequential. More specifically, it is shown that such patterns fall into the subsequential or reverse subsequential classes if the copying (for both cases) and deletion (for the case of metathesis only) are bounded in the right ways.

The classification of natural language patterns by the Chomsky Hierarchy (Chomsky, 1956) is one means of distinguishing the complexity of the patterns found in various linguistic domains. Syntactic patterns, for example, may be context-free (e.g. English nested embedding, (Chomsky, 1956)) or context-sensitive (e.g. Swiss German crossing dependencies (Schieber, 1985)), while phonological patterns (i.e. patterns that can be described with rewrite rules of the form A $\Rightarrow$ B / C __ D, where A, B, C, and D are regular expressions) have been shown by Johnson (1972) and Kaplan and Kay (1994) to be regular.

The regular class of patterns, however, is in fact too large to correspond exactly to phonology (Heinz, 2007; Heinz, 2009; Heinz, 2010). Rather, it seems that phonological patterns fit into a subclass of the regular patterns. Since the *subsequential class* is a proper subset of the regular class (Oncina et al., 1993; Mohri, 1997), it is therefore a useful candidate, especially because of its attractive computational properties (Mohri, 1997). Restricting the class of phonological patterns in this way has implications for learning, since the subsequential but not the regular class is identifiable in the limit from positive data (Oncina et al., 1993).

Using the formalism of finite state transducers (FSTs), we will show that metathesis and partial reduplication patterns can be described with subsequential FSTs. Subsequential FSTs are deterministic weighted transducers in which the weights are strings and multiplication is concatenation.

The analysis defines generally the conditions necessary for metathesis and partial reduplication to be subsequential. Representative examples of the empirical phenomena that can be so classified are shown in (1). (1-a) is an example of local metathesis, (1-b) is an example of metathesis around an intervening segment, and (1-c) is an example of partial reduplication.

*We thank the anonymous reviewers for useful questions and suggestions.This research is supported by grant #1035577 from the National Science Foundation.

(1) a. Rotuman:
hosa ⇒ hoas 'flower'
b. Cuzco Quechua:
yuraq ⇒ ruyaq 'white'
c. Tagalog:
sulat ⇒ susulat 'will write'

This kind of analysis sheds light on the nature of the relation itself independent of the particular theory used to account for it. It does not matter whether the metathesized or reduplicated forms exemplified here are derived via a series of SPE-style rules or with ranked constraints in OT. The mapping (e.g. <hosa, hoas> for Rotuman) remains the same in either case. Additionally, the analysis has implications for any model beyond the phonological domain that uses finite-state methodology, including (but not limited to) artificial intelligence (Russell and Norvig, 2009), bioinformatics (Durbin et al., 1998), natural language processing (Jurafsky and Martin, 2008), and robotics (Belta et al., 2007; Tanner et al., 2012).

The structure of the paper is as follows. Section two provides the formal definitions necessary for the analysis. Section three presents an analysis of subsequential copying, and section four presents an analysis of subsequential deletion. Section five turns to the analysis of metathesis as the composition of copying and deletion and proves the conditions for metathesis to be subsequential. Section six extends this analysis to partial reduplication. Section seven discusses the implications of the distinctions drawn by the computational analysis for both typology and learning. Section eight concludes.

2 Preliminaries

If Σ is a fixed finite set of symbols (an *alphabet*), then Σ^* is the set of all finite length strings formed over this alphabet, and $\Sigma^{\leq k}$ is the set of all strings of length less than or equal to *k*. A language is a subset of Σ^*. ϵ is the empty string. The length of a string s is $|s|$; thus $|\epsilon| = 0$. The *prefixes* of a string *s*, written $Pr(s)$, are $\{u \in \Sigma^* : \exists v \in \Sigma^* \text{ such that } s = uv\}$. The *suffixes* of a string *s*, written $Suf(s)$, are $\{u \in \Sigma^* : \exists v \in \Sigma^* \text{ such that } s = vu\}$. $Suf_n(s)$ is a suffix of *s* of length *n*. The nonempty, proper prefixes of a string s is written $Pr_{\text{prop}}(s)$.

If L is a language then the prefixes of L are $Pr(L) = \bigcup_{s \in L} Pr(s)$ and the nonempty proper prefixes of L are $Pr_{\text{prop}}(L) = \bigcup_{s \in L} Pr_{\text{prop}}(s)$. A language L is finite iff there exists some k such that $L \subseteq \Sigma^{\leq k}$. For any $w \in \Sigma^*$, the *good tails* of w in L is $T_L(w) = \{v \in \Sigma^* | wv \in L\}$. Two prefixes u_1 and u_2 are Nerode equivalent with respect to some language L iff they share the same good tails: $u_1 \sim_L u_2 \Leftrightarrow T_L(u_1) = T_L(u_2)$. In fact, a language L is *regular* iff the partition induced over Σ^* by $\sim_L$ has finite cardinality. Note that every finite language is regular. If L_1 and L_2 are languages then $L_1 L_2 = \{uv \mid u \in L_1 \text{ and } v \in L_2\}$.

Definition 1. *(Oncina et al., 1993) A* subsequential finite state transducer (SFST) *is a six-tuple (Q, Σ, Δ, q_0, δ, σ), where Q is a finite set of states, Σ is the input alphabet, Δ is the output alphabet, $q_0 \in Q$ is the initial state, $\delta \subset (Q \times \Sigma \times \Delta^* \times Q)$ is the transition function, and σ: $Q \Rightarrow \Delta^*$ is a partial function that assigns strings to the states in Q. The edges, E, of the SFST are a finite subset of $(Q \times \Sigma^* \times \Delta^* \times Q)$. SFSTs are deterministic, meaning they are subject to the condition $(q,a,u,r),(q,a,v,s) \in E \Rightarrow (u=v \wedge r=s)$.*

Definition 2. *(Oncina et al., 1993) A* path *in an SFST τ is a sequence of edges in τ, $\pi = (q_0, x_1, y_1, q_1)(q_1, x_2, y_2, q_2) \cdots (q_{n-1}, x_n, y_n, q_n)$. Π_τ is the set of all possible paths over τ. A path π can also be expressed as (q_0, x, y, q_n) where x $= x_1 x_2 ... x_n$ and y $= y_1 y_2 \cdots y_n$. The transduction τ realizes is the function t: $\Sigma^* \Rightarrow \Delta^*$ such that $\exists(q_0,x,y,q) \in \Pi_\tau$ and $t(x) = y\sigma(q)$.*

A relation describable with an SFST is a subsequential relation. If *f* and *g* are relations, $\circ$ denotes the composition, where $(g \circ f)(x) = g(f(x))$. Subsequential relations are closed under composition:

Theorem 1 ((Mohri, 1997) Theorem 1)**.** *Let f : $\Sigma^* \Rightarrow \Delta^*$ and g : $\Delta^* \Rightarrow \Omega^*$ be subsequential functions, then $g \circ f$ is subsequential.*

Let R be a relation. The reverse relation $R^r = \{<x^r, y^r>: <x,y> \in R\}$. A relation is reverse subsequential if its reverse relation is subsequential.

3 Subsequential copying

This paper will ultimately prove the conditions under which metathesis and partial reduplication, two processes which can be analyzed as involving copying, are subsequential relations. To do this it is first necessary to define a copy relation in general. A copy can be place either before or after the original—these two processes can be distinguished as pre-pivot or post-pivot copying (where the pivot is an intervening string from the set U).

Definition 3. *Let L,U,X,R be languages.*

1. *The rule* $\emptyset \Rightarrow X$ */ LXU__ R is a* post-pivot *copy relation.*

2. *The rule* $\emptyset \Rightarrow X$ */ L__ UXR is a* pre-pivot *copy relation.*

Kaplan and Kay (1994) show that if $L, X, U,$ and R are regular languages, then the copy relations above are regular relations. One goal of this paper is to identify the conditions on $L, X, U,$ and R which make the above relations subsequential.

Further distinctions can be drawn among regular copy relations based on which of the surrounding contexts of the copy and original are of bounded length.

Definition 4. *Let* $L, X, U,$ *and* R *be regular languages.*

1. *A pre-pivot or post-pivot copy relation is* I-bounded *iff U is a finite language (I is for 'intervening').*

2. *A pre-pivot copy relation is* L-bounded *iff L is a finite language (L is for 'left-context').*

3. *A post-pivot copy relation is* R-bounded *iff R is a finite language (R is for 'right-context').*

4. *A copy relation is* T-bounded *iff X is a finite language (T is for 'target').*

Theorem 2 below states that a pre-pivot, T-bounded, I-bounded, and R-bounded copy relation is subsequential. To understand the idea behind the proof, consider the abstract pre-pivot relation schematized in the following SFST for a particular $l \in L$, $u \in U$, $x \in X$, and $r \in R$.[1] Note that each transition in the figure represents a series of transitions and states (depending on the lengths of the strings involved).

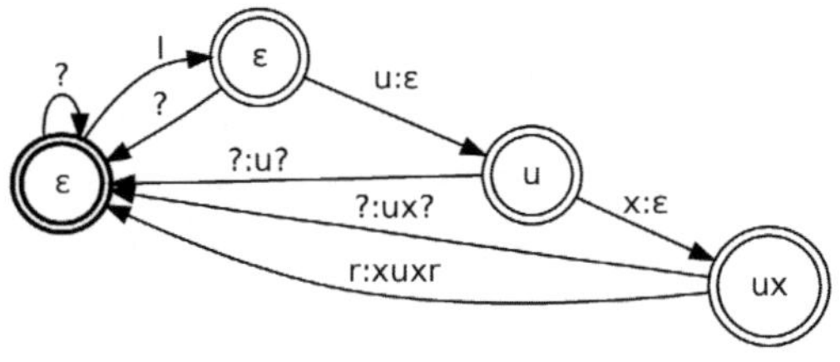

Figure 1: An SFST schematizing a pre-pivot T-bounded, I-bounded, and R-bounded copy relation.

The transitions for which the output is the empty string can be thought of as the machine withholding the output until it verifies that it has found the context for copying. Thus, out of the state labelled 'ux' the output on 'r' is 'xuxr', which is the copy followed by the segments for which there was no output (i.e. the segments in *u* and *x* that were being 'held'). This mechanism of holding is why the bounds on the lengths of the strings are necessary. If there were no upper bound on the length of the words in $U, X,$ or R, the machine would have to hold a potentially infinite number of strings, which would in turn require infinitely many states. Without these bounds, no SFST can be constructed.

Theorem 2. *A regular pre-pivot copy relation that is T-bounded, I-bounded, and R-bounded is subsequential.*

Proof. Let C be a pre-pivot, T-bounded, I-bounded, and R-bounded regular copy relation. Then there exists a regular language L and finite languages U, X, and R such that C is described by the rewrite rule $\emptyset \Rightarrow$ X / L__ UXR.

An SFST is constructed for C as follows. The states Q are the set of good tails of L and the non-empty proper prefixes of UXR. Formally, let $\pi_L = \{T_L(w) \mid w \in Pr(L)\}$. Then

$$Q = (\pi_L \cup Pr_{\text{prop}}(UXR))$$

Since L is a regular language, there are finitely many elements of π_L. Since $U, X,$ and R are finite lan-

[1] Following (Beesley and Karttunen, 2003), in this and all other FSTs in the paper, '?' represents any symbol or string except for those for which other transitions out of that state are defined. The states of the machine are labeled with the string mapped to them by the σ function.

guages, $Pr_{\text{prop}}(UXR)$ is also finite. Therefore Q is finite.

The initial state $q_0 = T_L(\epsilon)$.

The sigma function is defined as follows. $\forall q \in Q$,

$$\sigma(q) = \begin{cases} \epsilon & \text{iff } q \in \pi_L \\ q & \text{otherwise} \end{cases}$$

The transition function is defined in two parts. First, for all $s \in Pr(L)$ and $a \in \Sigma$:

$(T_L(s), a, a, T_L(sa)) \in E$ iff $s, sa \in Pr(L)$ and $s \notin L$
$(T_L(s), a, \epsilon, a) \in E$ iff $s \in L$ and $a \in Pr(UXR)$
$(T_L(s), a, a, T_L(\epsilon)) \in E$ otherwise

Second, for all s in the nonempty proper prefixes of UXR and $a \in \Sigma$:

$(s, a, \epsilon, sa) \in E$ iff $s, sa \in Pr_{\text{prop}}(UXR)$
$(s, a, xuxra, T_L(\epsilon)) \in E$ iff $(\exists x \in X)$ $(\exists u \in U)(\exists r \in Pr_{\text{prop}}(R))[s = uxr, ra \in R]$
$(s, a, \sigma(s)a, T_L(\epsilon)) \in E$ otherwise

It follows directly from this construction that the SFST recognizes the specified copy relation. □

Theorem 3 below states that a post-pivot copy relation need only be T- and R-bounded to be subsequential. The idea behind the proof is demonstrated by the abstract post-pivot copy relation schematized in the following SFST for a particular *x*, *u*, and *r*.

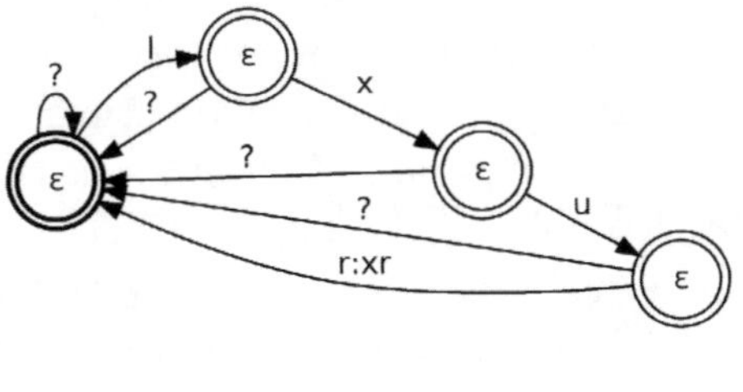

Figure 2: An SFST for a post-pivot T-bounded and R-bounded copy relation.

Since the machine finds the original *x* before it has to produce the copy, the segments in *u* do not have to be held. The bounding is only necessary for *x* itself, and for the right context of the copy *r*. Thus when the original precedes the copy, the bounding on *u* is no longer a necessary condition for subsequentiality.

Theorem 3. *A regular post-pivot copy relation that is T-bounded and R-bounded is subsequential.*

The proof of the Theorem 3 (omitted) is similar to the one for Theorem 2 but slightly more complicated by the fact that U can be any regular language.

The reverse of the relation in the proof of Theorem 3 would be a pre-pivot copy relation that is T-bounded and L-bounded. This would reverse the pattern in Figure 2, except the left context and not the right context would be bounded. Such a pattern is not subsequential, but it is reverse subsequential.

Corollary 1. *A regular pre-pivot copy relation that is T-bounded and L-bounded is reverse subsequential.*

4 Subsequential deletion

As with copying, the deletion relations relevant for metathesis come in two flavors, depending on whether the deleted string precedes or follows the one that remains.

Definition 5. *Let L,U,X,R be languages.*

1. *The rule X ⇒ ∅ / LXU__ R is a* post-pivot *deletion relation.*
2. *The rule X ⇒ ∅ / L__ UXR is a* pre-pivot *deletion relation.*

Kaplan and Kay (1994) show that if L, X, U, and R are regular languages, then the deletion relations above are regular relations. Another goal of this paper is to identify the conditions on L, X, U, and R which make the relations above subsequential.

We can thus provide parallel definitions for T-bounded, I-bounded, and R-bounded deletion relations.

Definition 6. *Let L,X,U,R be regular languages.*

1. *A pre-pivot or post-pivot deletion relation is* I-bounded *iff U is a finite language.*
2. *A pre-pivot deletion relation is* L-bounded *iff L is a finite language.*
3. *A post-pivot deletion relation is* R-bounded *iff R is a finite language.*
4. *A deletion relation is* T-bounded *iff X is a finite language.*

Figure 3 schematizes a pre-pivot regular deletion relation that is T-bounded, I-bounded, and R-bounded.

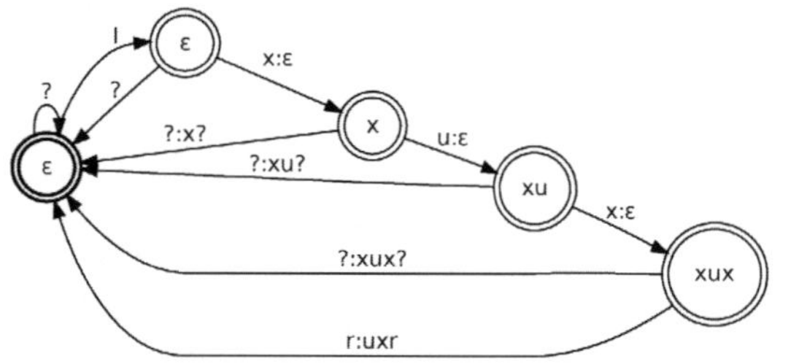

Figure 3: An SFST for a pre-pivot T-bounded, I-bounded, and R-bounded deletion relation.

As with the copying, due to the need for ϵ-transitions, the possibility of constructing this machine depends on the bounding of the length of the deleted string, the intervening string, and the string that makes up the right context.

Theorem 4. *A regular pre-pivot deletion relation that is T-bounded, I-bounded, and R-bounded is subsequential.*

Proof. Let D be a pre-pivot, T-bounded, I-bounded, and R-bounded regular deletion relation. Then there exists a regular language L and finite languages X, R, and U such that D is defined by the rewrite rule X $\Rightarrow$ $\emptyset$ / L__ UXR.

An SFST is constructed for D as follows. The states Q are the set of good tails of L and the nonempty proper prefixes of XUXR. Formally, let $\pi_L = \{T_L(w) \mid w \in Pr(L)\}$. Then

$$Q = (\pi_L \cup Pr_{\text{prop}}(XUXR))$$

Since L is regular, π_L is finite. Since U, X, and R are finite languages, $Pr_{\text{prop}}(XUXR)$ is also finite. Therefore Q is finite.

The initial state $q_0 = T_L(\epsilon)$. The sigma function is defined as in Theorem 2.

Also as in Theorem 2, the transition function is defined in two parts. The first part, where all $s \in Pr(L)$ and $a \in \Sigma$ are considered, is the same as in Theorem 2 except for one case below.

$$(T_L(s), a, \epsilon, a) \in E \quad \text{iff} \quad s \in L \text{ and } a \in Pr(XUXR)$$

The second part, where all s in the nonempty proper prefixes of XUXR and $a \in \Sigma$ are considered, is constructed as follows.

$$(s, a, \epsilon, sa) \in E \text{ iff } s, sa \in Pr_{\text{prop}}(XUXR)$$
$$(s, a, uxra, T_L(\epsilon)) \in E \text{ iff}(\exists x, x' \in X)$$
$$(\exists u \in U)(\exists r \in Pr_{\text{prop}}(R))[s = xux'r, ra \in R]$$
$$(s, a, \sigma(s)a, T_L(\epsilon)) \in E \text{ otherwise}$$

It follows directly from this construction that the SFST recognizes the deletion relation D. □

As for a post-pivot deletion relation, the properties of T-bounding and R-bounding are sufficient for subsequentiality since the intervening set U occurs before the deletion. As with Theorem 3, the proof of Theorem 5 is omitted.

Theorem 5. *A regular post-pivot deletion relation that is T-bounded and R-bounded is subsequential.*

Lastly, if *u* is not bounded in a pre-pivot deletion relation, but *l* and *x* are, the relation is reverse subsequential.

Corollary 2. *A regular pre-pivot deletion relation that is T-bounded and L-bounded is reverse subsequential.*

5 Metathesis as the composition of copying and deletion

Metathesis has traditionally been viewed as an operation of transposition, in which segments switch positions. Under another view, metathesis can be considered as the result of two separate processes, a copy process followed by deletion of the original segment the copy was made from (Blevins and Garrett, 1998; Blevins and Garrett, 2004). Take, for example, the metathesis process in Najdi Arabic (Abboud, 1979) in which a word with a CaCCat template surfaces as CCaCat:

(2) /naʕɟat/ $\Rightarrow$ [nʕaɟat] 'ewe'

An independent process of deletion (CaCaC $\Rightarrow$ CCaC) is also observed in Arabic dialects. So the change in (2) could be achieved via the two processes in (3). The result after both processes corresponds to metathesis (4).

(3) a. Copy: $\mathbf{CV_1CC} \Rightarrow \mathrm{CV_1CV_1C}$
b. Delete: $\mathrm{CV_1CV_1C} \Rightarrow \mathbf{CCV_1C}$

(4) Metathesis: $\mathbf{CV_1CC \Rightarrow CCV_1C}$

This analysis provides a way of classifying attested patterns according to the type of copying and deletion involved. Cross-linguistic surveys (Blevins and Garrett, 1998; Blevins and Garrett, 2004; Hume, 2000; Buckley, 2011; Chandlee et al., to appear) reveal that in a large number of metathesis patterns there is some bound on the length of the string that intervenes between the copied segment and its original. A classic example is found in the Rotuman language, in which the incomplete form of a word is derived from the complete form via word-final consonant-vowel metathesis (Churchward, 1940). The general rule for the example in (5-a) is in (5-b).

(5) a. hosa ⇒ hoas 'flower'
b. CV ⇒ VC / V __ #

If we decompose this metathesis into its component copy and deletion operations, the copy portion would be as in (6):[2]

(6) $V_1CV_2\# \Rightarrow V_1V_2CV_2\#$

Applying Definitions 3 and 4 to this example, we first classify the Rotuman pattern as pre-pivot copying. Since the length of the string between the original segment and the copy (u = C) is bounded by 1, the copying is I-bounded. The copying is also T-bounded, since a single vowel is copied ($x = V_2$). And it is R-bounded, since the original vowel is word-final ($r = \epsilon$). An FST for this pattern is shown in Figure 4. Note that when the right context is the empty string, the copying is achieved via the σ function rather than a transition.

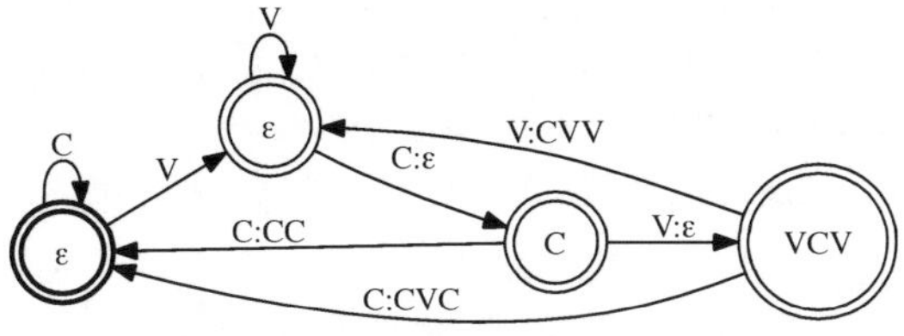

Figure 4: An SFST for the copy process of Rotuman CV-metathesis.

[2]This analysis assumes that it is the vowel that metathesizes. The same surface form would obtain if the consonant metathesized ($C_1V \Rightarrow C_1VC_1 \Rightarrow VC_1$). For evidence that the vowel is indeed the segment involved in CV metathesis, see (Heinz, 2005).

Another example of I-bounded copying is in an optional metathesis process in Cuzco Quechua, in which sonorants metathesize across an intervening vowel (Davidson, 1977):

(7) yuraq ⇒ ruyaq 'white'

Under a copy+deletion analysis of metathesis, this pattern would involve two copy processes followed by two deletions, one for the 'r' and one for the 'y'. Schematizing just the process for 'r', we can see in (8) that the length of the intervening string is again bounded by 1 (the 'y' is removed for clarity).[3] The copied string x (the liquid) is also bound by 1.

(8) uraq ⇒ ruraq

L-bounded copying is exemplified in a diachronic metathesis pattern found in a South Italian dialect of Greek (Rohlfs, 1950):

(9) Classical South Italian Greek
gambros ⇒ grambo[4] 'son-in-law'

In this pattern, a non-initial liquid surfaces in the initial onset cluster. The original position of the liquid varies, which means there is no bound on the length of the intervening string. However, the location of the copy is always the initial cluster, which means the left context of the copy *is* bounded by the length of the maximum onset.

The copying in metathesis is only the first step - the second is deletion of the original. The deletion rule must be complementary to the copying, in the sense that if the copying is pre-pivot, the deletion will be post-pivot (10), and vice versa (11).

(10) a. Copy: ∅ ⇒ x / v__ uxw
b. Delete: x ⇒ ∅ / vxu __ w

(11) a. Copy: ∅ ⇒ x / vxu __ w
b. Delete: x ⇒ ∅ / v__ uxw

As stated in section 2, if two relations are subsequential, then the composition of these relations will also be subsequential. Thus, whether or not the metathesis is subsequential depends on its component copy and deletion processes. This result is es-

[3]This assumes the two copy-deletions occur simultaneously. If one were to precede the other, then the bound would be 2.

[4]The [s] is deleted in an unrelated process.

tablished in the following theorem.

Theorem 6. *If a copy relation* f *is either (1) post-pivot, T-bounded, I-bounded and R-bounded or (2) pre-pivot, T-bounded, and R-bounded, and a deletion relation* g *is either (1) post-pivot, T-bounded, I-bounded and R-bounded or (2) pre-pivot, T-bounded, and R-bounded, then the metathesis relation* g ∘ f *is subsequential.*

Proof. By Theorems 2 and 3, f is subsequential. By Theorems 4 and 5, g is subsequential. By Theorem 1, $g \circ f$ is subsequential. □

6 Partial Reduplication

Unlike metathesis, reduplication is analyzed by phonologists of all stripes as involving copying. Traditionally, two categories of reduplication have been described: full (or total) and partial. Full reduplication involves copying the entire string and affixing it to the original. A classic example is found in Indonesian (Sneddon, 1996), to express the plural:

(12) a. buku 'book'
b. buku-buku 'books'

In contrast, partial reduplication involves copying a designated portion of the string and affixing it as either a prefix, suffix, or infix. These options can be schematized as in (13)(Riggle, 2003), in which local means the reduplicant attaches adjacent to the material it copies and nonlocal means the reduplicant copies a non-adjacent portion of the string:[5]

(13) a. local prefixation: CV-CVZ
b. nonlocal prefixation: CV-ZCV
c. local suffixation: ZCV-CV
d. nonlocal suffixation: CVZ-CV
e. infixation: C_1VC_1Z

An example of local prefixation is found in Tagalog, in which the future of a verb is derived from the stem with a CV reduplicative prefix (Blake, 1917):

(14) sulat ⇒ susulat 'will write'

An example of the infixation shown in (13-e) can be found in Pima, in which the plural is derived by infixing a copy of the initial consonant after the first vowel (Riggle, 2006):

(15) sipuk ⇒ sispuk 'cardinals'

Since under the current analysis of metathesis as copy+delete, the only difference between a metathesis pattern and partial reduplication is that the latter does not involve the second process of deletion, we should predict that partial reduplication patterns will also be subsequential if the copying is bounded as per the definitions given above. We can clearly see that in the local patterns (13-a) and (13-c), the original and the copy are adjacent and therefore (vacuously) they are I-bounded. For the infixation, the copy likewise appears at a fixed distance from the original. In all three cases, the amount of material to be copied fits a template and is thus bounded by the length of the template (i.e. they are T-bounded). Therefore by Theorem 2, these partial reduplication patterns are subsequential. The SFST for local prefixation (13-a) is shown in Figure 5.

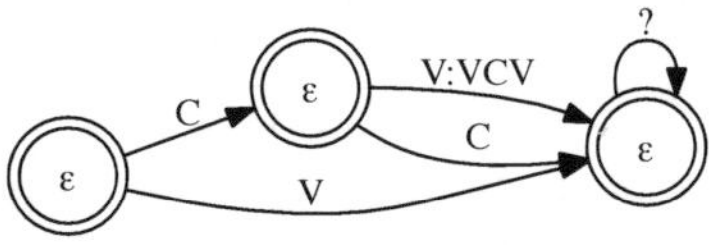

Figure 5: An SFST for CV-CVZ partial reduplication.

The SFST for local suffixation (13-c) is shown in Figure 6.

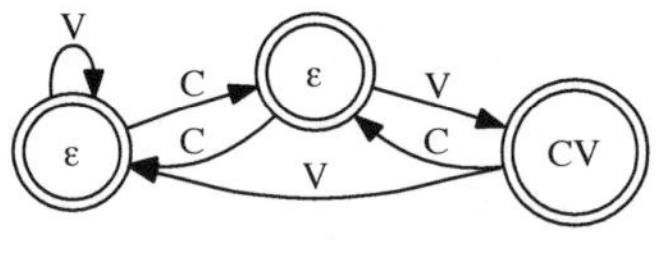

Figure 6: An SFST for ZCV-CV partial reduplication.

And the SFST for infixation (13-e) is shown in Figure 7.

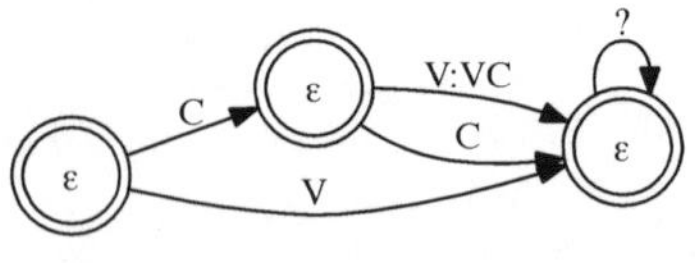

Figure 7: An SFST for C_1VC_1Z partial reduplication.

As for the nonlocal patterns, first consider the case of suffixation, (13-d). The string represented by Z

[5] These schemas assume CV reduplication, but the analysis would proceed the same for any reduplicant template, CC, CVC, etc.

is not bounded, and therefore this pattern is not I-bounded. It is, however, R-bounded, since the copy is always affixed to the end of the word. The right context is the empty string, which is (vacuously) bounded. Thus, by Theorem 3 this pattern is also subsequential; the FST is presented in Figure 8.

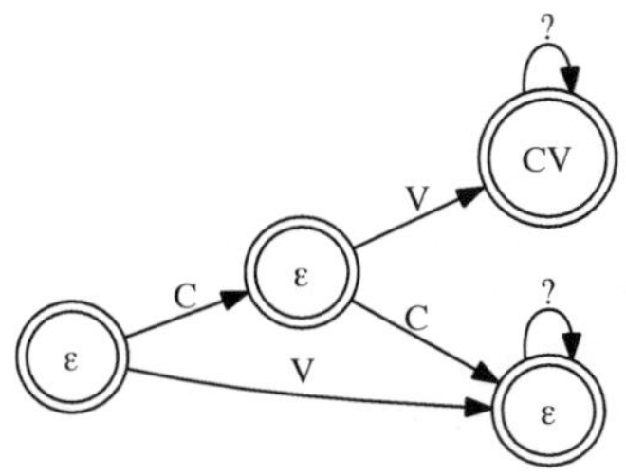

Figure 8: An SFST for a CVZ-CV pattern.

As for the last pattern, nonlocal prefixation, we have the opposite situation: the machine does have to hold a potentially infinite number of segments while it searches for the original, which means the pattern is not subsequential. However, this partial reduplication pattern is reverse subsequential by Corollary 1: reversing the string CV-ZCV gives VCZ-VC, which is R-bounded and identical to the nonlocal suffixation that was already argued to be subsequential.

To summarize, the attested partial reduplication patterns all appear to be subsequential or reverse subsequential.

This leaves us with full reduplication. Full reduplication is non-regular—although the position of the copy is fixed, the amount of material that is copied is not: full reduplication is not T-bounded. Again, with no principled upper limit on the length of words, a machine that copies an entire string cannot be finite state, much less subsequential. This distinction separates full and partial reduplication in terms of computational complexity—the implication being that these processes may be better viewed as distinct phenomena rather than subclasses of a single process.

7 Discussion

The analyses of subsequential copying and deletion presented above have revealed the conditions under which metathesis and partial reduplication patterns are subsequential. Under a copy+deletion analysis of metathesis, all metathesis patterns are T-bounded, since only one segment is copied (and then deleted) at a time. Partial reduplication is also T-bounded, assuming what is copied fits a certain template. Thus the T-bounded requirement on subsequential copying excludes only full reduplication from the subsequential class.

The analysis of metathesis relied on generalized representations of such patterns that appear to be typologically justified. A large number of attested metathesis patterns are considered 'local', which amounts to being I-bounded by 1. Metathesis patterns described as 'long distance' are also either I-bounded or else L-bounded - patterns such as Romance liquid movement (Vennemann, 1988) and Romani aspiration displacement (Matras, 2002) are striking in that they all affect the initial onset of the word.[6] A type of logically possible pattern that appears to be unattested is one in which no context of the copying - left, right, or intervening - is bounded. Such a pattern would not be subsequential, and in fact could not be described with any FST (i.e. it is non-regular). In this way the restriction of metathesis to the subsequential class finds support in the typological evidence. Also (apparently) unattested is an R-bounded metathesis pattern - one which targets the end of the word - though this is readily found in the typology of partial reduplication. It remains for future work whether such a metathesis pattern does exist, and if not, whether further distinctions need to be drawn to account for why R-bounded copying only appears as partial reduplication.

Narrowing the computational bound of possible phonological patterns from the regular class to the subsequential class also has implications for learning. It is known that the class of regular languages is not identifiable in the limit from positive data (Gold, 1967), but the subsequential class is: Oncina et al. (1993) have shown this class to be learnable by the OSTIA algorithm. Although (without modification) OSTIA does not do so well in practice on real data sets (Gildea and Jurafsky, 1996), future work may reveal algorithms that fare better if the hypothesis space can be restricted even further (i.e. to a sub-

[6]The L-bounded patterns also appear to be restricted to the diachronic domain. See (Chandlee et al., to appear)

class of the subsequential relations).

8 Conclusion

This paper has argued for an analysis of metathesis as the composition of copying and deletion. Such an analysis provides a computational link between metathesis and partial reduplication, which extends into a classification of these patterns as subsequential based on the bounded nature of the copying and (in the case of metathesis) deletion. The typology of attested patterns aligns well with the classifications proposed here, suggesting a tighter computational bound on phonological patterns than the one established by Johnson (1972) and Kaplan and Kay (1994).

Thus we can add metathesis and partial reduplication to the phonological processes that have previously been shown to be subsequential - see (Koirala, 2010) for substitution, insertion, and deletion, and Gainor et al. (to appear) for vowel harmony. It will be interesting to see to what extent morphological processes, including templatic morphology, and prosodic circumscription, also fit into this class.

References

P. F. Abboud. 1979. The verb in Northern Najdi Arabic. *Bulletin of the School of Oriental and African Studies*, 42:467-499.

K.R. Beesley and L. Karttunen. 2003. *Finite State Morphology.* Stanford: CSLI Publications.

C. Belta, A. Bicchi, M. Egerstedt, E. Frazzoli, E. Klavins and G. J. Pappas. 2007 Symbolic planning and control of robot motion. *IEEE Robotics and Automation Magazine*, 14(1): 61–71.

F. R. Blake. 1917. Reduplication in Tagalog. *The American Journal of Philology*, 38: 425-431.

J. Blevins and A. Garrett. 1998. The origins of consonant-vowel metathesis. *Language*, 74(3):508-556.

J. Blevins and A. Garrett. 2004. The evolution of metathesis. In B. Hayes, R. Kirchner, and D. Steriade (eds.) *Phonetically Based Phonology*. Cambridge: Cambridge UP, 117-156.

E. Buckley. 2011. Metathesis. In M. van Oostendorp, C.J. Ewen, E. Hume, and K. Rice (eds.) *The Blackwell Companion to Phonology*, Volume 3. Wiley-Blackwell.

J. Chandlee, A. Athanasopoulou, and J. Heinz. to appear Evidence for classifying metathesis patterns as subsequential. *Proceedings of the 29th West Coast Conference on Formal Linguistics* Somerville: Cascadilla.

N. Chomsky. 1956. Three models for the description of language. *IRE Transactions on Information Theory 113124.* IT-2.

C. M. Churchward. 1940. *Rotuman grammar and dictionary*. Sydney: Methodist Church of Australasia, Department of Overseas Missions.

J. O. Davidson, Jr. 1977. A Contrastive Study of the Grammatical Structures of Aymara and Cuzco Quechua Ph.D. dissertation. University of California, Berkeley.

R. Durbin, S. R. Eddy, A. Krogh, and G. Mitchison 1998 *Biological Sequence Analysis: Probabilistic Models of Proteins and Nucleic Acids* Cambridge University Press.

B. Gainor, R. Lai, and J. Heinz. to appear Computational characterizations of vowel harmony patterns and pathologies. *Proceedings of the 29th West Coast Conference on Formal Linguistics.* Somerville: Cascadilla.

D. Gildea and D. Jurafsky. 1996. Learning bias and phonological-rule induction. *Computational Linguistics*22, 497-530.

E.M. Gold. 1967. Language identification in the limit. *Infomation and Control*10, 447-474.

J. Heinz. 2005. Optional partial metathesis in Kwara'ae. *Proceedings of AFLA 12, UCLA Working Papers*, 91-102.

J. Heinz. 2007. The inductive learning of phonotactic patterns. Doctoral dissertation, University of California, Los Angeles.

J. Heinz. 2009. On the role of locality in learning stress patterns. *Phonology* 26: 303-351.

J. Heinz. 2010. Learning long-distance phonotactics. *Linguistic Inquiry* 41, 623-661.

E. Hume. 2000. *Metathesis Website*. www.ling.ohio-state.edu/ ehume/metathesis.

C. D. Johnson. 1972. *Formal Aspects of Phonological Description* The Hague: Mouton.

D. Jurafsky and J.H. Martin 2008 *Speech and Language Processing, 2nd edition.* Pearson Prentice Hall.

R. Kaplan and M. Kay. 1994. Regular models of phonological rules systems. *Computational Linguistics* 20: 331-378.

C. Koirala. 2012. Strictly Local Relations. Ms. University of Delaware.

Y. Matras. 2002. *Romani: a linguistic introduction.* Cambridge: Cambridge UP.

M. Mohri. 1997. Finite-state transducers in language and speech processing. *Computational Linguistics*, 23: 269-311.

J. Oncina, P. Garcia, and E. Vidal. 1993. Learning subsequential transducers for pattern recognition interpretation tasks. *IEEE Transactions on Pattern Analysis and Machine Intelligence*, 15(5): 448-457.

J. Riggle. 2003. Nonlocal reduplication. *Proceedings of the 34th annual meeting of the North Eastern Linguistic Society*.

J. Riggle. 2006. Infixing reduplication in Pima and its theoretical consequences. *Natural Language and Linguistic Theory*, 24: 857-891.

G. Rohlfs. 1950. *Historische grammatik der unteritalienischen Gräzität*, München: Verlag der Bayerischen Akademie der Wissenchaften.

S. Russell and P. Norvig. 2009 *Artificial Intelligence: a modern approach.* Upper Saddle River, NJ: Prentice Hall

S. Schieber. 1985 Evidence against the context-freeness of natural language. *Linguistics and Philosophy* 8: 333-343.

J. N. Sneddon. 1996. *Indonesian: a comprehensive grammar*, Routledge.

H. G. Tanner, C. Rawal, J. Fu, J. L. Piovesan, and C. T. Abdallah. 2012 Finite abstractions for hybrid systems with stable continuous dynamics. *Discrete Event Dynamic Systems* ,22(1):83-99.

T. Vennemann. 1988. *Preference laws for syllable structure and the explanation of sound change.* Berlin: Mouton de Gruyter.

An approximation approach to the problem of the acquisition of phonotactics in Optimality Theory

Giorgio Magri
Laboratoire de Linguistique Formelle, CNRS and University of Paris 7
magrigrg@gmail.com

Abstract

The *problem of the acquisition of phonotactics* in Optimality Theory is intractable. This paper offers a way to cope with this hardness result: the problem is reformulated as a well known integer program (the *Assignment problem* with *linear side constraints*) paving the way for the application to phonotactics of *approximation algorithms* recently developed for integer programming.

Knowledge of the *phonotactics* of a language is knowledge of its distinction between licit and illicit forms. The acquisition of phonotactics represents a distinguished and important stage of language acquisition. In fact, in carefully controlled experimental conditions, nine-month-old infants already react differently to licit and illicit sound combinations (Jusczyk et al., 1993). They thus display knowledge of phonotactics already at an early stage of language development.

Usually, the problem of the acquisition of the phonotactics of a language given a finite set of linguistic data is formalized as the problem of finding a smallest language in the typology that is consistent with the data (Berwick, 1985; Manzini and Wexler, 1987; Prince and Tesar, 2004; Hayes, 2004; Fodor and Sakas, 2005). Section 1 formulates the problem of the acquisition of phonotactics along these lines within the mainstream phonological framework of *Optimality Theory* (Prince and Smolensky, 2004; Kager, 1999).

Unfortunately, (such a formulation of) the problem of the acquisition of phonotactics in OT turns out to be intractable (NP-complete): for any attempted efficient solution algorithm, there are some instances of the problem where the algorithm fails (Magri, 2010; Magri, 2012b). This hardness result holds for the *universal* formulation of the problem, in the sense of Heinz et al. (2009): there are no restrictions on the constraint set that defines the OT typology and indeed the OT typology itself figures as an input to the problem.

There are two strategies to cope with this hardness result. One approach weakens the formulation of the problem through proper restrictions on the constraint set: certain constraint sets are implausible from a phonological perspective, and should therefore be ignored in the proper formulation of the problem (Magri, 2011; Magri, 2012c). This approach raises interesting challenges, as it requires a through investigation of the algorithmic implications of various generalizations developed by phonologists on what counts as a "plausible" OT constraint set. Another approach is to bypass this difficulty, and weaken the formulation of the problem by lowering the standard for success: we settle on an *approximate* solution, namely a "small" language rather than a smallest language. This paper paves the way for the latter approach.

I focus on the specific formulation of the problem of the acquisition of OT phonotactics developed in Prince and Tesar (2004). In Sections 2 and 3, I show that this formulation of the problem can be restated as a classical integer program, namely the *Assignment problem* with *liner side constraints* (AssignLSCsPbm). The theory of *approximation algorithms* for integer programing is a blooming field of Computer Science (Bertsimas and Weismantel, 2005). In particular, powerful approximation algorithms have been recently developed for the AssignLSCsPbm. A state-of-the-art algorithm is due to Arora et al. (2002). The integer programming formulation developed in this paper thus paves the way for a new approximation approach to the problem of modeling the acquisition of phonotactics within OT. In Magri (2012a), I report simulation results with Arora's et. al. (2002) algorithm on various instances of the problem of the acquisition of phonotactics.

1 Formulation of the problem

1.1 Basic formulation

A *typology* in Optimality Theory (OT) is defined through a 4-tuple $\tau = (\mathcal{X}, \mathcal{Y}, Gen, \mathfrak{C})$, where $\mathcal{X}$ is the set of *underlying forms*; $\mathcal{Y}$ is the set of *candidate surface forms*; Gen is the *generating function* that pairs an underlying form $x \in \mathcal{X}$ with a set $Gen(x) \subseteq \mathcal{Y}$ of surface forms called the *candidates* for x; and $\mathfrak{C}$ is the set of n *constraints* $C_1, \ldots, C_n$. Each constraint C_i is a function that maps a pair (x, y) of an underlying form $x \in \mathcal{X}$ and a candidate $y \in Gen(x)$ into a number $C_i(x, y)$, called the corresponding *number of violations*. The constraint set is split into the subset $\mathcal{M}$ of markedness constraints and the subset $\mathcal{F}$ of *faithfulness constraints*. As the constraint set is finite and can therefore only distinguish among a finite number of forms, I can assume that the set of underlying forms $\mathcal{X}$ is finite, as well as the candidate set $Gen(x)$ for any underlying form $x \in \mathcal{X}$.

Let π be a *ranking*, namely a total order over the constraint set. I denote by $\mathsf{OT}_\pi\colon \mathcal{X} \to \mathcal{Y}$ the *OT grammar* corresponding to the ranking π, as defined in Prince and Smolensky (2004). And I denote by $\mathcal{L}(\pi)$ the language corresponding to the ranking π, namely the range of the corresponding grammar OT_π (or, more explicitly, the set of all and only those surface forms $\hat{y} \in \mathcal{Y}$ such that there exists an underlying form $x \in \mathcal{X}$ such that $\mathsf{OT}_\pi(x) = \hat{y}$). Throughout the paper, I use x for an underlying form, $\hat{y}$ for a surface form which is an intended winner, and y for a surface form which is an intended loser.

The *Problem of the acquisition of phonotactics* in OT can be stated as in (1) in its universal formulation (Berwick, 1985; Manzini and Wexler, 1987; Prince and Tesar, 2004; Hayes, 2004). We are given an OT typology as well as a finite set $P \subseteq \mathcal{X} \times \mathcal{Y}$ of linguistic data. These data consist of pairs $(x, \hat{y})$ of an underlying form $x \in \mathcal{X}$ and a corresponding intended winner form $\hat{y} \in Gen(x)$. I assume that P is *consistent*, namely that there exists at least a ranking π such that $\mathsf{OT}_\pi(x) = \hat{y}$ for every pair $(x, \hat{y}) \in P$. We are asked to return a ranking π which has two properties. First, π is *consistent*: the corresponding OT grammar maps x into $\hat{y}$ for every pair $(x, \hat{y}) \in P$. Second, π is *restrictive*: there exists no other ranking π' consistent with P too such that the language $\mathcal{L}(\pi')$ corresponding to π' is a proper subset of the language $\mathcal{L}(\pi)$ corresponding to π. A solution algorithm needs to run in time polynomial in the number of constraints $|\mathfrak{C}|$ and the numbers of forms $|\mathcal{X}|, |\mathcal{Y}|$ (recall that $\mathcal{X}$ and $\mathcal{Y}$ are finite).

(1) *given*: an OT typology $\tau = (\mathcal{X}, \mathcal{Y}, Gen, \mathfrak{C})$ and a finite set $P \subseteq \mathcal{X} \times \mathcal{Y}$ of data;
find: a ranking π s.t. $P \subseteq \mathsf{OT}_\pi$ and there is no π' s.t. $P \subseteq \mathsf{OT}_{\pi'}$ and $\mathcal{L}(\pi') \subset \mathcal{L}(\pi)$;
time: $\max\{|\mathfrak{C}|, |\mathcal{X}|, |\mathcal{Y}|\}$.

Problem (1) is NP-complete: there exists no efficient algorithm that is able to solve any instance of the problem (Magri, 2010; Magri, 2012b).

An interesting variant of the problem (1) assumes that we are given only the surface forms but not the corresponding underlying forms. Prince and Tesar (2004) and Hayes (2004) suggest that we can circumvent this difficulty as follows. Assume that the set of underlying forms and the set of surface forms coincide, namely $\mathcal{X} = \mathcal{Y}$. Assume furthermore that the typology is *output driven* (Tesar, 2008): a surface form $\hat{y}$ belongs to the language $\mathcal{L}(\pi)$ corresponding to a ranking π iff the corresponding grammar OT_π maps that form $\hat{y}$ (construed as an underlying form) into itself (construed as a surface form), as stated in (2)

$$(2) \quad \hat{y} \in \mathcal{L}(\pi) \iff \mathsf{OT}_\pi(\hat{y}) = \hat{y}.$$

In this case, a way to cope with the lack of the underlying forms is to assume that the underlying form corresponding to a given surface form $\hat{y}$ is the completely faithful underlying form $\hat{y}$ itself. For this reason, I stick with the formulation (1) of the problem, whereby we are provided with both surface and underlying forms.

1.2 ERC notation

Consider an underlying form $x \in \mathcal{X}$ and two different candidate forms $y, \hat{y} \in Gen(x)$, with the convention that $\hat{y}$ is the intended winner for x while y is a loser. Following Prince (2002), all the relevant information concerning the underlying/winner/loser form triplet $(x, \hat{y}, y)$ can be summarized into the corresponding *elementary ranking condition* (ERC), namely the n-tuple $\mathbf{e}$ with entries $e_1, \ldots, e_n \in \{\text{L}, e, \text{W}\}$ defined as in (3).

$$(3) \quad (x, \hat{y}, y) \implies \mathbf{e} = \boxed{e_1 \mid \ldots \mid e_i \mid \ldots \mid e_n}$$

$$e_i \doteq \begin{cases} \text{W} & \text{if } C_i(x, \hat{y}) < C_i(x, y) \\ \text{L} & \text{if } C_i(x, \hat{y}) > C_i(x, y) \\ e & \text{if } C_i(x, \hat{y}) = C_i(x, y) \end{cases}$$

In words, The ith entry e_i is $e_i = \text{W}$ iff constraint C_i assigns more violations to (x, y) than to $(x, \hat{y})$ and thus favors the intended winner $\hat{y}$ over the loser y; $e_i = \text{L}$ iff the opposite holds; finally, $e_i = e$ iff the constraint C_i assigns the same number of violations to the two pairs (x, y) and $(x, \hat{y})$.

A ranking π can be represented as a permutation over $\{1, \ldots, n\}$, with the understanding that $\pi(i) = j$ means that the ranking π assigns constraint C_i to the jth stratum of the ranking, with the convention that the stratum corresponding to $j = n$ (to $j = 1$) is the top (bottom) of the ranking. For every such permutation π, let $\mathbf{e}_\pi$ be the n-tuple $\mathbf{e}$ with the components reordered according to π in decreasing order, as in (4).

(4) $$\mathbf{e}_\pi \doteq (e_{\pi(n)}, \ldots, e_{\pi(1)})$$

The ERC $\mathbf{e}$ is *OT-consistent* with π provided the left-most component of $\mathbf{e}_\pi$ different from e is a W.

For each of the pairs $(x, \hat{y})$ in the set P given with an instance of the problem (1), consider each loser candidate $y \in Gen(x)$ different from $\hat{y}$, construct the ERC corresponding to the underlying/winner/loser form triplet $(x, \hat{y}, y)$ as in (3) and organize all these ERCs one underneath the other into an *ERC matrix* with n columns and many rows (the order of the ERCs does not matter). I denote a generic ERC matrix by $\mathbf{E}$ and I say that a ranking π is *OT-consistent* with $\mathbf{E}$ provided it is consistent with each of its ERCs. The problem of the acquisition of phonotactics in (1) can thus be equivalently restated in ERC notation as in (5).

(5) *given*: an OT typology $\tau = (\mathcal{X}, \mathcal{Y}, Gen, \mathfrak{C})$ and an ERC matrix $\mathbf{E}$;
find: a ranking π s.t. π is OT-consistent with $\mathbf{E}$ and there is no π' consistent with $\mathbf{E}$ too s.t. $\mathcal{L}(\pi') \subset \mathcal{L}(\pi)$;
time: $\max\{|\mathfrak{C}|, |\mathcal{X}|, |\mathcal{Y}|\}$.

The latter formulation of the problem is only partially stated in terms of ERC notation, as the condition $\mathcal{L}(\pi') \subset \mathcal{L}(\pi)$ still requires knowledge of the entire OT typology. This difficulty is tackled in the next Subsection.

1.3 Restrictiveness measures

Let a *restrictiveness measure* be a function μ which takes a ranking π and returns a number $\mu(\pi) \in \mathbb{N}$ that provides a relative measure of the size of the language $\mathcal{L}(\pi)$ corresponding to π, in the sense that the (strict) monotonicity property in (6) holds for any two rankings π, π'.

(6) If $\mathcal{L}(\pi') \subset \mathcal{L}(\pi)$, then $\mu(\pi') < \mu(\pi)$.

Any solution of the optimization problem (7) is a solution of the corresponding instance (5) of the problem of the acquisition of phonotactics. In fact, if π solves (7) then there cannot exist any other ranking π' consistent with the ERC matrix that corresponds to a smaller language $\mathcal{L}(\pi') \subset \mathcal{L}(\pi)$, since (6) would imply that $\mu(\pi') < \mu(\pi)$, contradicting the hypothesis that π is a solution of (7).

(7) *minimize*: $\mu(\pi)$;
subject to: π is OT-consistent with the given ERC matrix $\mathbf{E}$;
time: number of columns and rows of $\mathbf{E}$.

As problem (7) is stated completely in terms of the ERC matrix $\mathbf{E}$, the time required by a solution algorithm needs to scale just with the size of $\mathbf{E}$.

From now on, I will focus on the new formulation (7). Thus, I need a restrictiveness measure (6). Of course, not just any restrictiveness measure will do. For instance, the function (8), which pairs a ranking π with the cardinality of its language $\mathcal{L}(\pi)$, trivially satisfies (6).

(8) $$\mu(\pi) \doteq |\mathcal{L}(\pi)|.$$

Yet, this is not a *good* restrictiveness measure, because there seems to be no way to compute $\mu(\pi)$ without actually computing the language $\mathcal{L}(\pi)$, which requires knowledge of the entire typology.

Prince and Tesar (2004) suggest a better candidate, which is defined for any ranking π as in (9). Recall that the constraint set $\mathfrak{C} = \mathcal{F} \cup \mathcal{M}$ is split up into the subset $\mathcal{F}$ of faithfulness constraints and the subset $\mathcal{M}$ of markedness constraints. For each faithfulness constraint $F \in \mathcal{F}$, determine the number $\mu(F)$ of markedness constraints $M \in \mathcal{M}$ ranked by π *below* that faithfulness constraint, i.e. $\pi(F) > \pi(M)$. Finally, add up all these numbers $\mu(F)$ together to determine the value $\mu(\pi)$.

(9) $$\mu(\pi) \doteq \sum_{F \in \mathcal{F}} \underbrace{\Big|\{M \in \mathcal{M} \,|\, \pi(F) > \pi(M)\}\Big|}_{\mu(F)}$$

Is the function μ defined in (9) is a restrictiveness measure? namely, does it satisfy condition (6)? Prince and Tesarconjecture that it is, based on the following intuition. Markedness (faithfulness) constraints work against (towards) the preservation of the underlying contrasts. Thus, a small (large) language should arise by ranking the markedness (faithfulness) constraints as high as possible. And a ranking that ranks the markedness (faithfulness) constraints as high (low) as possible is a ranking that minimizes Prince and Tesar's function (9).

I endorse Prince and Tesar's conjecture that (9) is a restrictiveness measure, at least for the cases of interest.[1] In Magri (2012a), I backup this claim by looking at a case study, namely the typology corresponding to the large constraint set considered in Pater and Barlow (2003). In the rest of this paper, I thus focus on the reformulation (7) of the problem of the acquisition of phonotactics, with μ defined as in (9). The latter formulation of the problem of the acquisition of phonotactics is NP-complete too (Magri, 2010; Magri, 2012b). In the rest of this paper, I thus develop an integer programming formulation of the latter problem, that allows approximation algorithms for integer programming to be used in order to tackle the problem of the acquisition of phonotactics. The reasoning is split up into two steps. In Section, 2, I develop an integer programming formulation of the objective function, namely the alleged restrictiveness measure in (9). And in Section 3, I turn to an integer programming formulation of the OT-consistency condition.

2 An integer programming restatement of the restrictiveness measure

A *square matrix of order* n is a collection of n^2 real numbers displayed into n columns and n rows. I denote a square matrix of order n as $\mathbf{X} = [x_{i,j}]_{i,j=1}^n$, with the understanding that $x_{i,j}$ is the element of the matrix $\mathbf{X}$ which sits in the ith row and the jth column. I denote by $\mathbb{R}^{n\times n}$ the vector space of all square matrices of order n.

A square matrix $\mathbf{X} = [x_{i,j}]_{i,j=1}^n$ is called a *permutation matrix* iff its elements $x_{i,j}$ satisfy the following three conditions: (i) they are all 0 or 1; (ii) each column contains a unique 1; (iii) each row contains a unique 1. I denote by $\mathcal{P}^n$ the set of all $n!$ permutation matrices of order n. To illustrate, I list $\mathcal{P}^n$ with $n = 3$ in (10).

(10)
$$\begin{bmatrix}1&0&0\\0&1&0\\0&0&1\end{bmatrix}\begin{bmatrix}1&0&0\\0&0&1\\0&1&0\end{bmatrix}\begin{bmatrix}0&1&0\\1&0&0\\0&0&1\end{bmatrix}$$
$$\begin{bmatrix}0&0&1\\1&0&0\\0&1&0\end{bmatrix}\begin{bmatrix}0&1&0\\0&0&1\\1&0&0\end{bmatrix}\begin{bmatrix}0&0&1\\0&1&0\\1&0&0\end{bmatrix}$$

Permutation matrices play a special role in convex geometry (Webster, 1984, par. 5.8).

There is a natural correspondence between permutation matrices of order n and rankings over n constraints $C_1, \ldots, C_n$. Recall that a ranking π is a permutation over $\{1, 2, \ldots, n\}$, with the understanding that $\pi(i) = j$ means that the ranking π assigns the constraint C_i to the jth stratum, with the convention that the stratum corresponding to $j = n$ is the top stratum. I use i as the index ranging over constraints and j as the index ranging over strata. Thus, a ranking π can be identified with that (unique) permutation matrix $\mathbf{X} = [x_{i,j}]_{i,j=1}^n \in \mathcal{P}^n$ such that $x_{i,j} = 1$ iff the ranking π assigns the constraint C_i to the jth stratum, namely $\pi(i) = j$. To illustrate, I list in (11) the rankings over $\{C_1, C_2, C_3\}$ corresponding to the six permutation matrices in (10), respectively.

(11) $C_3 \gg C_2 \gg C_1$, $C_2 \gg C_3 \gg C_1$, $C_3 \gg C_1 \gg C_2$,
$C_1 \gg C_3 \gg C_2$, $C_2 \gg C_1 \gg C_3$, $C_1 \gg C_2 \gg C_3$

I denote by $\pi_{\mathbf{X}}$ the ranking corresponding to a permutation matrix $\mathbf{X} \in \mathcal{P}^n$ and by $\mathbf{X}_\pi \in \mathcal{P}^n$ the permutation matrix corresponding to a ranking π. Prince and Tesar's restrictiveness measure (9) of a ranking π can be straightforwardly read off the corresponding permutation matrix $\mathbf{X}_\pi$, as follows.

Define the *scalar product* $\langle \mathbf{X}, \mathbf{Y} \rangle \in \mathbb{R}$ between two arbitrary square matrices $\mathbf{X} = [x_{i,j}]_{i,j=1}^n, \mathbf{Y} = [y_{i,j}]_{i,j=1}^n \in \mathbb{R}^{n\times n}$ as in (12) (namely as the Euclidean scalar product of $\mathbb{R}^{n^2}$).

[1] Prince and Tesar's conjecture that (9) is a restrictiveness measure runs into a straightforward problem when the constraint set $\mathfrak{C}$ contains both positional and faithfulness constraints. Yet, there are various ways to circumvent this difficulty posed by positional constraints. One way could be to weigh differently the two types of faithfulness constraints in the determination of restrictiveness. Thus, we could switch from the definition in (9) to the variant in (i), where $\mathcal{F}_{pos}$ is the set of positional faithfulness constraints, $\mathcal{F}_{gen}$ is the set of general faithfulness constraints and α is a positive coefficient.

(i) $$\mu_\alpha(\pi) \doteq \sum_{F\in\mathcal{F}_{pos}} \left|\left\{M \in \mathcal{M} \,\middle|\, \pi(F) > \pi(M)\right\}\right| + \alpha \sum_{F\in\mathcal{F}_{gen}} \left|\left\{M \in \mathcal{M} \,\middle|\, \pi(F) > \pi(M)\right\}\right|$$

Another way to deal with positional faithfulness constraints could be to ignore altogether rankings where a positional faithfulness constraint is ranked below the corresponding general faithfulness constraint. This is trivial to obtain, by adding a proper ERC to the ERC matrix given with an instance of the problem (7).

(12) $\langle \mathbf{X}, \mathbf{Y} \rangle \doteq \sum_{i,j=1}^{n} x_{i,j} y_{i,j}.$

A function $f : \mathbb{R}^{n \times n} \longrightarrow \mathbb{R}$ is called *linear* iff there exists a square matrix $\mathbf{\Sigma} \in \mathbb{R}^{n \times n}$ such that (13) holds for any square matrix $\mathbf{X} \in \mathbb{R}^{n \times n}$.

(13) $f(\mathbf{X}) = \langle \mathbf{\Sigma}, \mathbf{X} \rangle.$

Linear functions are the "simplest" possible convex functions, namely the ones that yield the easiest optimization problems.

Let me assume that the first m constraints in $\mathfrak{C}$ are the faithfulness constraints while the remaining $n - m$ constraints are the markedness constraints, namely that $\mathcal{F} = \{C_1, \ldots, C_m\}$ and $\mathcal{M} = \{C_{m+1}, \ldots, C_n\}$. Consider the matrix $\mathbf{\Sigma}_{n,m} \in \mathbb{R}^{n \times n}$ defined as follows: its first m rows each have the form $[0, 1, \ldots, n-2, n-1]$; the remaining $n - m$ rows are all null. To illustrate, I give in (14) the matrix $\mathbf{\Sigma}_{n,m}$ with $n = 7, m = 4$.

(14) $$\mathbf{\Sigma}_{7,4} \doteq \left[\begin{array}{ccccccc} 0 & 1 & 2 & 3 & 4 & 5 & 6 \\ 0 & 1 & 2 & 3 & 4 & 5 & 6 \\ 0 & 1 & 2 & 3 & 4 & 5 & 6 \\ 0 & 1 & 2 & 3 & 4 & 5 & 6 \\ \hline 0 & 0 & 0 & 0 & 0 & 0 & 0 \\ 0 & 0 & 0 & 0 & 0 & 0 & 0 \\ 0 & 0 & 0 & 0 & 0 & 0 & 0 \end{array}\right]$$

The following Claim 1 explains how to compute the restrictiveness $\mu(\pi)$ of a ranking π according to (9) out of the corresponding permutation matrix $\mathbf{X}_\pi$; see Appendix A.1. This Claim shows an important property of Prince and Tesar's restrictiveness measure: it can be described as a linear function over the set of permutation matrices.

Claim 1 *The restrictiveness $\mu(\pi)$ of a ranking π according to (9) can be computed as follows:*

(15) $\mu(\pi) = \langle \mathbf{\Sigma}_{n,m}, \mathbf{X}_\pi \rangle - \frac{1}{2} m(m-1)$

namely as the scalar product $\langle \mathbf{\Sigma}_{n,m}, \mathbf{X} \rangle$ between the matrix $\mathbf{\Sigma}_{n,m}$ and the corresponding permutation matrix $\mathbf{X}_\pi$, minus the constant $\frac{1}{2}m(m-1)$ which does not depend on the ranking.[2] ■

The problem of the acquisition of phonotactics (7) with Prince and Tesar's alleged restrictiveness measure (9) can thus be restated as the optimization problem (16).

(16) *minimize*: $\langle \mathbf{\Sigma}_{n,m}, \mathbf{X} \rangle$;
subject to: $\mathbf{X} \in \mathcal{P}^n$ and $\pi_{\mathbf{X}}$ is consistent with the given ERC matrix $\mathbf{E}$.

Here, I have dropped the constant $\frac{1}{2}m(m-1)$ which appears in (15), as it does not affect the optimization problem.

3 An integer programming formulation of the OT-consistency condition

The reformulation in (16) makes use of the notion of OT-consistency with a given ERC matrix and this notion is currently stated in terms of rankings rather than in terms of the corresponding permutation matrices. We need to restate the latter condition directly in terms of permutation matrices. In this Section, I point out two strategies for doing that. The first approach hinges on a classical observation by Prince and Smolensky (2004) that OT consistency can be restated as linear consistency in the case of exponentially spaced weights. The second approach requires a larger number of linear conditions, but is shown to provide a better reformulation (i.e. a tighter relaxation).

3.1 An initial formulation of OT-consistency

Given an ERC $\mathbf{e} = [e_1, \ldots, e_n]$, consider the corresponding square matrix $\mathbf{A}_\mathbf{e} = [a_{i,j}]_{i,j=1}^n \in \mathbb{R}^{n \times n}$ defined in (17). Here, t_i is the *sign* of the ERC's entry e_i, namely t_i is equal to -1, 0 or $+1$ depending on whether e_i is equal to L, e or W. Thus, the entry $a_{i,j}$ in the ith row and the jth column of the matrix (17) consists of the sign t_i multiplied by 2^j.

(17) $$\mathbf{A}_\mathbf{e} = \begin{bmatrix} 2^1 t_1 & 2^2 t_1 & \ldots & 2^j t_1 & \ldots & 2^n t_1 \\ & & & \vdots & & \\ 2^1 t_i & 2^2 t_i & \ldots & 2^j t_i & \ldots & 2^n t_i \\ & & & \vdots & & \\ 2^1 t_n & 2^2 t_n & \ldots & 2^j t_n & \ldots & 2^n t_n \end{bmatrix}$$

Intuitively, this entry $a_{i,j} = 2^j t_i$ is the weight of the sign t_i under the assumption that the constraint

[2] I have noted in footnote 1 that the conjecture that the function μ in (9) is a restrictiveness measure runs into problems for constraint sets that contain both general and positional faithfulness constraints. And I have suggested that a possible way out is to to switch from the definition (9) to the variant in (i). Let me now point out that the latter variant too can be described as a linear function over permutation matrices. In fact, let $\mathbf{\Sigma}_{n,m,\alpha}$ be as the matrix $\mathbf{\Sigma}_{n,m}$ defined above, but with the rows corresponding to general faithfulness constraints multiplied by α. Then, $\mu_\alpha(\mathbf{X})$ coincides with $\langle \mathbf{\Sigma}_{n,m,\alpha}, \mathbf{X} \rangle$, but for a constant.

C_i is assigned to the jth stratum.

The following claim offers a restatement of OT-consistency between an ERC and a ranking in terms of the permutation matrix corresponding to that ranking. This claim is just a restatement in matrix form of the observation by Prince and Smolensky (2004) that OT consistency is equivalent to a linear condition with exponentially spaced weights; see Subsection A.2.

Claim 2 *A ranking π is OT-consistent with an ERC* $\mathbf{e}$ *iff $\langle \mathbf{A_e}, \mathbf{X}_\pi \rangle \geq 0$, where $\langle \mathbf{A_e}, \mathbf{X}_\pi \rangle$ is the scalar product (12) between the matrix $\mathbf{A_e}$ corresponding to the ERC* $\mathbf{e}$ *and the permutation matrix $\mathbf{X}_\pi$ corresponding to the ranking π.* ■

The current formulation (16) of the problem of the acquisition of phonotactics can thus be restated as the optimization problem in (18).

(18) FIRST INTEGER REFORMULATION:

minimize: $\langle \mathbf{\Sigma}_{n,m}, \mathbf{X} \rangle$;

subject to: $\mathbf{X} \in \mathcal{P}^n$ s.t. $\langle \mathbf{A_e}, \mathbf{X} \rangle \geq 0$ for every ERC $\mathbf{e}$ of the ERC matrix $\mathbf{E}$.

Problem (18) is an optimization problem over permutation matrices $\mathbf{X} \in \mathcal{P}^n$. The *objective function* is the linear function $\langle \mathbf{\Sigma}_{n,m}, \mathbf{X} \rangle$. And the feasible set is defined in terms of linear *side conditions* $\langle \mathbf{A_e}, \mathbf{X} \rangle \geq 0$. Problem (18) is thus an *integer program*. In particular, it is an *Assignment problem* with *linear side constraints* (AssignLSCsPbm) (Bertsimas and Weismantel, 2005).

3.2 Another formulation of OT-consistency

Let $\ell(\mathbf{e})$ be the number of entries equal to L in an ERC $\mathbf{e} = [e_1, \ldots, e_n]$. Assume without loss of generality that $\ell(\mathbf{e}) > 0$, as ERCs with no L's can be ignored. For every stratum $\bar{\jmath} \in \{1, \ldots, n\}$, consider the square matrix $\mathbf{A}_\mathbf{e}^{\bar{\jmath}} = [a_{i,j}]_{i,j=1}^n$ with n rows and n columns whose generic element $a_{i,j}$ is defined as in (19).

(19)
$$a_{i,j} \doteq \begin{cases} 1 & \text{if } e_i = \text{L},\ j \geq \bar{\jmath} \\ -1 & \text{if } e_i = \text{W},\ j \geq \bar{\jmath} + \ell \\ 0 & \text{otherwise} \end{cases}$$

The following claim offers another restatement of OT-consistency between an ERC and a ranking in terms of the permutation matrix corresponding to that ranking; see Subsection A.3.

Claim 3 *A ranking π is OT-consistent with an ERC* $\mathbf{e}$ *iff $\langle \mathbf{A}_\mathbf{e}^{\bar{\jmath}}, \mathbf{X}_\pi \rangle \leq 0$ for every $\bar{\jmath} \in \{1, \ldots, n\}$, where $\langle \mathbf{A}_\mathbf{e}^{\bar{\jmath}}, \mathbf{X}_\pi \rangle$ is the scalar product (12) between the matrix $\mathbf{A}_\mathbf{e}^{\bar{\jmath}}$ corresponding to the ERC* $\mathbf{e}$ *and the stratum $\bar{\jmath}$ and the permutation matrix $\mathbf{X}_\pi$ corresponding to the ranking π.* ■

The current formulation (16) of the problem of the acquisition of phonotactics can thus be alternatively restated as the optimization problem (20).

(20) SECOND INTEGER REFORMULATION:

minimize: $\langle \mathbf{\Sigma}_{n,m}, \mathbf{X} \rangle$;

subject to: $\mathbf{X} \in \mathcal{P}^n$ s.t. $\langle \mathbf{A}_\mathbf{e}^{\bar{\jmath}}, \mathbf{X} \rangle \leq 0$ for every ERC $\mathbf{e}$ of the ERC matrix $\mathbf{E}$ and every $\bar{\jmath} \in \{1, \ldots, n\}$.

Again, (20) is another instance of the AssignLSCsPbm. The feasible set in the latter formulation (20) involves n times more inequalities than the formulation (18).

3.3 Comparing the two formulations

Problems (18) and (20) are two different formulations of the original problem (16) of the acquisition of phonotactics. They are thus equivalent, in the sense that a solution to any of the two problems is also a solution to the other and furthermore to the original problem. This Subsection explains why, nonetheless, the latter formulation (20) is better than the former formulation (18).

Both (18) and (20) are optimization problems over permutation matrices $\mathbf{X} \in \mathcal{P}^n$. The latter condition on the matrix $\mathbf{X} = [x_{i,j}]_{i,j=1}^n$ means that conditions (21) hold for any $i, j = 1, \ldots, n$.

(21)
$$x_{i,j} \in \{0, 1\}$$
$$\sum_{i=1}^n x_{i,j} = 1, \quad \sum_{j=1}^n x_{i,j} = 1$$

Problems (18) and (20) are *integer* optimization problems because of the condition $x_{i,j} \in \{0, 1\}$ in (21). This condition can be *relaxed*, requiring the entires $x_{i,j}$ to be not necessarily 0 or 1 but instead any number in between 0 and 1. Thus, let $\mathcal{P}_{\text{rel}}^n$ be the set of matrices that satisfy the relaxed conditions (22), known as the *Birkhoff polytope*.

(22)
$$x_{i,j} \in [0, 1]$$
$$\sum_{i=1}^n x_{i,j} = 1, \quad \sum_{j=1}^n x_{i,j} = 1$$

Relaxing the integer constraint $\mathbf{X} \in \mathcal{P}^n$ into the continuous constraint $\mathbf{X} \in \mathcal{P}_{\text{rel}}^n$, yields the two corresponding problems (23) and (24).

(23) First relaxation:

minimize: $\langle \mathbf{\Sigma}_{n,m}, \mathbf{X} \rangle$;

subject to: $\mathbf{X} \in \mathcal{P}^n_{\text{rel}}$ s.t. $\langle \mathbf{A_e}, \mathbf{X} \rangle \leq 0$ for any ERC $\mathbf{e}$ of the ERC matrix.

(24) Second relaxation:

minimize: $\langle \mathbf{\Sigma}_{n,m}, \mathbf{X} \rangle$;

subject to: $\mathbf{X} \in \mathcal{P}^n_{\text{rel}}$ s.t. $\langle \mathbf{A}^{\overline{\jmath}}_{\mathbf{e}}, \mathbf{X} \rangle \geq 0$ for any ERC $\mathbf{e}$ of the ERC matrix and any stratum $\overline{\jmath} \in \{1, \ldots, n\}$.

These linear programs (23) and (24) are the *relaxations* of the two integer programs (18) and (20).

The relaxation of an integer program provides a lower bound on the solution of that integer program. This lower bound is used by solution algorithms for the integer program. Of course, linear relaxations that provide tight bounds yield improved solution algorithms for the original integer problem (Bertsimas and Weismantel, 2005). Despite the fact that the two original integer programs (18) and (20) are equivalent, the two corresponding relaxations (23) and (24) are not. Claim 4 ensures that the feasible set of the relaxation (24) is a subset of that of the relaxation (23), so that the lower bound provided by a solution of the former will be at least as tight as the lower bound provided by a solution of the latter.

Claim 4 *If a matrix* $\mathbf{X}$ *belongs to the feasible set of problem (24), then it also belongs to the feasible set of problem (23).* ■

The following counterexample shows that the lower bound provided by the relaxation (24) is not just as tight as but actually tighter than the bound provided by the relaxation (23). Given the ERC matrix (25), the solution to the corresponding problem (7) is the ranking $F_2 \gg M \gg F_1$: the faithfulness constraint F_1 is redundant and should therefore be ranked at the bottom.

(25) $$\mathbf{E} = \begin{bmatrix} \text{W} & \text{W} & \text{L} \\ e & \text{W} & \text{L} \end{bmatrix}$$ (columns: F_1, F_2, M)

The solutions of the two corresponding relaxations (23) and (24) are provided in (26).[3]

(26) $$\mathbf{X}_{(23)} = \begin{matrix} F_1 \\ F_2 \\ M \end{matrix}\begin{bmatrix} 1 & 0 & 0 \\ 0 & \frac{1}{2} & \frac{1}{2} \\ 0 & \frac{1}{2} & \frac{1}{2} \end{bmatrix} \quad \mathbf{X}_{(24)} = \begin{matrix} F_1 \\ F_2 \\ M \end{matrix}\begin{bmatrix} 1 & 0 & 0 \\ 0 & 0 & 1 \\ 0 & 1 & 0 \end{bmatrix}$$ (columns: $st1$, $st2$, $st3$)

The relaxation (23) has a non-integral solution; the relaxation (24) is thus stronger because its solution is integral. The latter solution indeed represents the desired ranking, as it assigns F_2 to the top 3rd stratum (because of the 1 in the second column and third row) and F_1 to the bottom 1st stratum (because of the 1 in the first row and first column).

4 Conclusion

In this paper, I have focused on Prince and Tesar's (2004) formulation (7) of the problem of the acquisition of phonotactics, in terms of the alleged restrictiveness measure (9). This problem is NP-complete. To cope with this hardness result, in this paper I have looked for an integer programming formulation of the latter problem. The formulation in (20) has emerged as the best formulation among those considered, namely the one that yields the tightest relaxation. This problem (20) is an instance of a classical integer program, namely the *Assignment problem* with *linear side constraints* (AssignLSCsPbm). The result obtained in this paper thus paves the way for the efficient application of approximation algorithms for the AssignLSCsPbm to the problem of the acquisition of phonotactics in OT. In Magri (2012a), I report simulation results with Arora's et. al. (2002) algorithm, a state-of-the-art approximation algorithm for the AssignLSCsPbm.

Acknowledgments

I wish to thank A. Albright for endless discussion on the problem of the acquisition of phonotactics. This work was supported in part by a 'Euryi' grant from the European Science Foundation to P. Schlenker, by a grant from the Fyssen Research Foundation, and by the LABEX-EFL grant.

Appendix: proof of the main results

A.1 Proof of claim 1

Consider the example of the permutation matrix $\mathbf{X}$ in (27). There are seven constraints (hence $n = 7$), four of which are faithfulness constraints (hence $m = 4$). I have fringed each row of $\mathbf{X}$ with the name of the constraint it corresponds to and I have

[3] These solutions have been computed with the Matlab codes `RelaxedSubPbmFirstFormulation.m` and `RelaxedSubPbmSecondFormulation.m`, that solve the two relaxations (23) and (24), respectively. These codes are available on the author's website. The two codes use the two subroutines `MatrixToVectorConverter.m` and `VectorToMatrixConverter.m`, that are available on the author's website too.

fringed each column of $\mathbf{X}$ with the stratum it corresponds to.

$$
(27)\quad \mathbf{X} = \begin{array}{c} \\ F_1 \\ F_2 \\ F_3 \\ F_4 \\ M_5 \\ M_6 \\ M_7 \end{array} \begin{array}{c} \begin{array}{ccccccc} st1 & st2 & st3 & st4 & st5 & st6 & st7 \end{array} \\ \left[\begin{array}{ccccccc} 0 & \mathbf{1} & 0 & 0 & 0 & 0 & 0 \\ 0 & 0 & 0 & 0 & 0 & \mathbf{1} & 0 \\ 0 & 0 & \mathbf{1} & 0 & 0 & 0 & 0 \\ 0 & 0 & 0 & 0 & 0 & 0 & \mathbf{1} \\ 0 & 0 & 0 & \mathbf{1} & 0 & 0 & 0 \\ \mathbf{1} & 0 & 0 & 0 & 0 & 0 & 0 \\ 0 & 0 & 0 & 0 & \mathbf{1} & 0 & 0 \end{array}\right] \end{array}
$$

As prescribed by our conventions, the first four rows correspond to the four faithfulness constraints, the bottom three rows correspond to the markedness constraints; the leftmost column corresponds to the bottom stratum and the rightmost column corresponds to the top stratum.

The ranking $\pi_{\mathbf{X}}$ that corresponds to $\mathbf{X}$ can be obtained as follows: the 1 in the first column of $\mathbf{X}$ says that the markedness constraint M_6 is assigned by $\pi_{\mathbf{X}}$ to the bottom stratum $j = 1$; the 1 in the second column of $\mathbf{X}$ says that the faithfulness constraint F_1 is assigned to the next stratum $j = 2$; and so on. Thus, $\pi_{\mathbf{X}}$ is the ranking (28).

(28) $F_4 \gg F_2 \gg M_7 \gg M_5 \gg F_3 \gg F_1 \gg M_6$

According to (9), the restrictiveness $\mu(\pi_{\mathbf{X}})$ of this ranking $\pi_{\mathbf{X}}$ is $8 = 3{+}3{+}1{+}1$: 3 markedness constraints underneath F_4, another 3 underneath F_2, 1 underneath and F_3 as all as underneath F_1. Here is a way to quickly compute this number directly from the permutation matrix $\mathbf{X}$.

Consider the matrix (29) obtained from the matrix (27) through the following two steps. *First*, all 1's which appear in the bottom three rows of $\mathbf{X}$ (and thus correspond to markedness constraints) are replaced with 0's.

$$
(29)\quad \begin{array}{c} \\ F_1 \\ F_2 \\ F_3 \\ F_4 \\ M_1 \\ M_2 \\ M_3 \end{array} \begin{array}{c} \begin{array}{ccccccc} st1 & st2 & st3 & st4 & st5 & st6 & st7 \end{array} \\ \left[\begin{array}{ccccccc} 0 & \mathbf{1} & 0 & 0 & 0 & 0 & 0 \\ 0 & 0 & 0 & 0 & 0 & \mathbf{5} & 0 \\ 0 & 0 & \mathbf{2} & 0 & 0 & 0 & 0 \\ 0 & 0 & 0 & 0 & 0 & 0 & \mathbf{6} \\ 0 & 0 & 0 & 0 & 0 & 0 & 0 \\ 0 & 0 & 0 & 0 & 0 & 0 & 0 \\ 0 & 0 & 0 & 0 & 0 & 0 & 0 \end{array}\right] \end{array}
$$

Second, each 1 which appears in one of the top four rows of $\mathbf{X}$ (and thus corresponds to a faithfulness constraint) is replaced with the number which identifes the corresponding column, diminished by 1. Thus for example, the 1 in the second row in the matrix $\mathbf{X}$ in (27) is replaced by a 5 in (29), since it occurs in the sixth column.

Next, let's scan the columns of the matrix (29) from left to right, assigning to each column which is not all zeros a progressive index k starting from $k = 0$, as made explicit in (30).

$$
(30)\quad \begin{array}{c} \\ F_1 \\ F_2 \\ F_3 \\ F_4 \\ M_1 \\ M_2 \\ M_3 \end{array} \begin{array}{c} \begin{array}{ccccccc} & k_1{=}0 & k_3{=}1 & & & k_2{=}2 & k_4{=}3 \end{array} \\ \left[\begin{array}{ccccccc} 0 & \mathbf{1} & 0 & 0 & 0 & 0 & 0 \\ 0 & 0 & 0 & 0 & 0 & \mathbf{5} & 0 \\ 0 & 0 & \mathbf{2} & 0 & 0 & 0 & 0 \\ 0 & 0 & 0 & 0 & 0 & 0 & \mathbf{6} \\ 0 & 0 & 0 & 0 & 0 & 0 & 0 \\ 0 & 0 & 0 & 0 & 0 & 0 & 0 \\ 0 & 0 & 0 & 0 & 0 & 0 & 0 \end{array}\right] \end{array}
$$

Now we can straightforwardly read out of (30) the number of markedness constraints ranked by $\pi_{\mathbf{X}}$ below each faithfulness constraint: F_1 has only one markedness constraint ranked below it, which is precisely the number $i_1 = 1$ which appears in the row corresponding to F_1 diminished by the value $k_1 = 0$ which corresponds to the column where that number appears; F_2 has three markedness constraints ranked below it, which is precisely the number $i_2 = 5$ which appears in the row corresponding to F_2 diminished by the value $k_2 = 2$ which corresponds to the column where that number appears; and so on.

Since $\mu(\pi_{\mathbf{X}})$ is defined in (9) as the sum over each faithfulness constraint of the number of markedness constraints ranked below that faithfulness constraint, we get the right result as in (31).

$$
\begin{aligned}
(31)\quad \mu(\pi_{\mathbf{X}}) &= \\
&= \mu(F_1) + \mu(F_2) + \mu(F_3) + \mu(F_4) \\
&= (i_1 - k_1) + (i_2 - k_2) + (i_3 - k_3) + (i_4 - k_4) \\
&= (1 - 0) + (5 - 2) + (2 - 1) + (6 - 3) \\
&= 8
\end{aligned}
$$

Note that the sum in the second line of (31) can be rearranged as follows:

$$
\begin{aligned}
(32)\quad \mu(\pi_{\mathbf{X}}) &= \\
&= (i_1 + i_2 + i_3 + i_4) - (k_1 + k_2 + k_3 + k_4) \\
&= (i_1 + i_2 + i_3 + i_4) - (0 + 1 + 2 + 3)
\end{aligned}
$$

It is trivial to check directly from the definition (12) of scalar product that the first term $i_1 + i_2 + i_3 + i_4$ in the second line of (32) is the scalar product $\langle \mathbf{\Sigma}_{7,4}, \mathbf{X} \rangle$ between the permutation matrix $\mathbf{X}$ in (27) and the matrix $\mathbf{\Sigma}_{7,4}$ in (14). Thus, the first term in the second line of (32) corresponds to the first term in (15). It is also trivial to check that the second term $0+1+2+3$ in the second line of (32) is equal to $\frac{1}{2}m(m-1)$ for $m=4$. Thus, the second term in the second line of (32) corresponds to the second term in (15).

A.2 Proof of claim 2

Consider a ranking π, namely a permutation over $\{1,\ldots,n\}$. Let π^{-1} be its inverse. Recall that $\pi(i)=j$ means that constraint C_i is assigned by the ranking π to the jth stratum, with the top stratum being the one corresponding to $j=n$. Thus, $\pi^{-1}(j)$ is the constraint assigned by π to the jth stratum. Given an ERC $\mathbf{e}=[e_1,\ldots,e_n]$, let $k=k(\mathbf{e})\in\{1,\ldots,n\}$ be univocally defined by conditions (33): they say that the constraints assigned by π to the top strata $k+1,\ldots,n$ all have an e in the ERC $\mathbf{e}$ so that the constraint assigned by π to the kth stratum is the highest one that does not have an e in the ERC.

(33) a. $e_{\pi^{-1}(k+1)}=\ldots=e_{\pi^{-1}(n)}=e.$
b. $e_{\pi^{-1}(k)}\neq e.$

Thus, π is OT-consistent with the ERC $\mathbf{e}$ iff $e_{\pi^{-1}(k)}=\text{W}$. To prove Claim 2, I thus prove the equivalence (34), where $\mathbf{X}_\pi=[x_{i,j}]_{i,j=1}^{n}$ is the permutation matrix corresponding to π and $\mathbf{A}_\mathbf{e}=[a_{i,j}]_{i.j=1}^{n}$ is the matrix defined in (17).

(34) $$\langle\mathbf{A}_\mathbf{e},\mathbf{X}_\pi\rangle>0\iff e_{\pi^{-1}(k)}=\text{W}.$$

Assume that $e_{\pi^{-1}(k)}=\text{W}$; then I can reason as follows, following Prince and Smolensky (2004):

(35) $$\begin{aligned}\langle\mathbf{A}_\mathbf{e},\mathbf{X}_\pi\rangle&=\sum_{i,j=1}^{n}x_{i,j}a_{i,j}&&=\sum_{i,j=1}^{n}x_{i,j}2^jt_i\\&=\sum_{i=1}^{n}t_i\sum_{j=1}^{n}x_{i,j}2^j&&=\sum_{i=1}^{n}t_i2^{\pi(i)}\\&=\sum_{j=1}^{n}t_{\pi^{-1}(j)}2^j&&>2^k-\sum_{j=1}^{k-1}2^j>0\end{aligned}$$

The proof of the reverse implication is analogous.

A.3 Proof of claim 3

To illustrate why claim 3 holds, consider the concrete case of the ERC $\mathbf{e}$ in (36).

(36) $$\mathbf{t}=\begin{bmatrix}\overset{C_1}{\text{W}}&\overset{C_2}{\text{W}}&\overset{C_3}{e}&\overset{C_4}{e}&\overset{C_5}{\text{L}}\end{bmatrix}$$

A ranking π is OT-consistent with this ERC $\mathbf{e}$ provided it ranks either C_1 or C_2 above C_5. This condition is equivalent to the set of implications (37). For example, the the third implication says that if, π assigns C_5 to either stratum 3, or 4 or 5 (the latter being the top stratum), then π must assign either C_1 or C_2 to either stratum 4 or 5.

(37) $$\begin{aligned}C_5\in\{1,2,3,4,5\}&\Longrightarrow C_1\in\{2,3,4,5\}&&\vee\ C_2\in\{2,3,4,5\}\\C_5\in\{2,3,4,5\}&\Longrightarrow C_1\in\{3,4,5\}&&\vee\ C_2\in\{3,4,5\}\\C_5\in\{3,4,5\}&\Longrightarrow C_1\in\{4,5\}&&\vee\ C_2\in\{4,5\}\\C_5\in\{4,5\}&\Longrightarrow C_1\in\{5\}&&\vee\ C_2\in\{5\}\\C_5\in\{5\}&\Longrightarrow C_1\in\emptyset&&\vee\ C_2\in\emptyset\end{aligned}$$

Consider the permutation matrix $\mathbf{X}=[x_{i,j}]_{i,j=1}^{n=5}$. Recall that $x_{i,j}=1$ iff the corresponding ranking π satisfies the condition $\pi(i)=j$ namely it assigns constraint C_i to the jth stratum. Thus, the implications in (37) can be restated in terms of permutation matrices rather than rankings as in (38), in the sense that a ranking π satisfies (37) iff the corresponding permutation matrix $\mathbf{X}_\pi$ satisfies (38). The five inequalities (38) can be written in

(38) $$\begin{aligned}x_{5,1}+x_{5,2}+x_{5,3}+x_{5,4}+x_{5,5}&\leq x_{1,2}+x_{1,3}+x_{1,4}+x_{1,5}+x_{2,2}+x_{2,3}+x_{2,4}+x_{2,5}\\x_{5,2}+x_{5,3}+x_{5,4}+x_{5,5}&\leq x_{1,3}+x_{1,4}+x_{1,5}+x_{2,3}+x_{2,4}+x_{2,5}\\x_{5,3}+x_{5,4}+x_{5,5}&\leq x_{1,4}+x_{1,5}+x_{2,4}+x_{2,5}\\x_{5,4}+x_{5,5}&\leq x_{1,5}+x_{2,5}\\x_{5,5}&\leq 0\end{aligned}$$

(39) $$2x_{5,1}+4x_{5,2}+8x_{5,3}+16x_{5,4}\leq 2x_{1,1}+4x_{1,2}+8x_{1,3}+16x_{1,4}+32x_{1,5}+2x_{2,1}+4x_{2,2}+8x_{2,3}+16x_{2,4}+32x_{2,5}$$

(40) $$\begin{aligned}4x_{5,1}+4x_{5,2}+4x_{5,3}+4x_{5,4}&\leq 4x_{1,2}+4x_{1,3}+4x_{1,4}+4x_{i,5}+4x_{2,2}+4x_{2,3}+4x_{2,4}+4x_{2,5}\\4x_{5,2}+4x_{5,3}+4x_{5,4}&\leq 4x_{1,3}+4x_{1,4}+4x_{1,5}+4x_{2,3}+4x_{2,4}+4x_{2,5}\\8x_{5,3}+8x_{5,4}&\leq 8x_{1,4}+8x_{1,5}+8x_{2,4}+8x_{2,5}\\16x_{5,4}&\leq 16x_{1,5}+16x_{2,5}\end{aligned}$$

(41) $$4x_{5,1}+8x_{5,2}+16x_{5,3}+32x_{5,4}\leq 4x_{1,2}+8x_{1,3}+16x_{1,4}+32x_{1,5}+4x_{2,2}+8x_{2,3}+16x_{2,4}+32x_{2,5}$$

matrix notation as $\langle \mathbf{A}_{\mathbf{e}}^{\bar{\jmath}}, \mathbf{X} \rangle \leq 0$ for $\bar{\jmath} = 1, \ldots, 5$.

A.4 Proof of claim 4

To illustrate why claim 4 holds, consider again the concrete case of the ERC (36). As just noted, the conditions $\langle \mathbf{A}_{\mathbf{e}}^{\bar{\jmath}}, \mathbf{X} \rangle \leq 0$ for $\bar{\jmath} = 1, \ldots, 5$ enforced by the relaxation (24) boil down to the inequalities (38). The condition $\langle \mathbf{A}_{\mathbf{e}}, \mathbf{X} \rangle \geq 0$ enforced by the relaxation (23) boils down to the inequality (39). In order to prove claim 4 in this specific case, I thus need to show that, if $\mathbf{X} \in \mathcal{P}_{\text{rel}}^{n}$ satisfies inequalities (38), then it also satisfies inequalities (39). Indeed, the last inequality in (38) says that $x_{5,5}$ is null, and can thus be dropped from the other four inequalities (38). Multiplying the first inequality in (38) by 4, the second by 4, the third by 8 and the fourth by 16, I get (40). Summing the inequalities (40) together, I get the inequality (41). As $x_{i,j} \geq 0$, I can weaken the inequality (41) by dividing the left hand side by 2 and by adding $2x_{1,1}$ and $2x_{2,1}$ to the right hand side, thus obtaining the desired inequality (39).

References

Sanjeev Arora, Alan Frieze, and Haim Kaplan. 2002. A New Rounding Procedure for the Assignment Problem with Applications to Dense Graph Arrangement Problems. *Mathematical Programming*, 92.1:1–36.

Dimitris Bertsimas and Robert Weismantel. 2005. *Optimization over Integers*. Dynamic Ideas, Belmont, Massachusetts.

Robert Berwick. 1985. *The acquisition of syntactic knowledge*. MIT Press, Cambridge, MA.

Janet Dean Fodor and William Gregory Sakas. 2005. The subset principle in syntax: costs of compliance. *Linguistics*, 41:513–569.

Bruce Hayes. 2004. Phonological Acquisition in Optimality Theory: The Early Stages. In R. Kager, J. Pater, and W. Zonneveld, editors, *Constraints in Phonological Acquisition*, pages 158–203. Cambridge University Press.

Jeffrey Heinz, Gregory M. Kobele, and Jason Riggle. 2009. Evaluating the Complexity of Optimality Theory. *Linguistic Inquiry*, 40:277–288.

P. W. Jusczyk, A. D. Friederici, J. M. I. Wessels, V. Y. Svenkerud, and A. Jusczyk. 1993. Infants' sensitivity to the sound patterns of native language words. *Journal of Memory and Language*, 32:402–420.

René Kager. 1999. *Optimality Theory*. Cambridge University Press.

Giorgio Magri. 2010. Complexity of the Acquisition of Phonotactics in Optimality Theory. In Jeffrey Heinz, Lynne Cahill, and Richard Wicentowski, editors, *Proceedings of SIGMORPHON 11: the 11th biannual meeting of the ACL Special Interest Group on Computational Morphology and Phonology*, pages 19–27, Uppsala, Sweden. Association for Computational Linguistics.

Giorgio Magri. 2011. An online model of the acquisition of phonotactics within Optimality Theory. In L. Carlson, C. Hölscher, and T. Shipley, editors, *Proceedings of CogSci 33: the 33rd annual conference of the Cognitive Science Society*, Austin, TX:. Cognitive Science Society.

Giorgio Magri. 2012a. An approximation approach to the problem of the acquisition of phonotactics in optimality theory. manuscript available on the author's website; this is a longer version of the present paper.

Giorgio Magri. 2012b. Complexity of the acquisition of Phonotactics in Optimality Theory. Accepted at *Linguistic Inquiry*.

Giorgio Magri. 2012c. Restrictiveness of error-driven ranking algorithms: an initial assessment. Manuscript in progress.

M. Rita Manzini and Ken Wexler. 1987. Parameters, Binding Theory, and Learnability. *Linguistic Inquiry*, 18.3:413–444.

Joe Pater and Jessica A. Barlow. 2003. Constraint conflict in cluster reduction. *Journal of Child Language*, 30:487–526.

Alan Prince and Paul Smolensky. 2004. *Optimality Theory: Constraint Interaction in Generative Grammar*. Blackwell. As Technical Report CU-CS-696-93, Department of Computer Science, University of Colorado at Boulder, and Technical Report TR-2, Rutgers Center for Cognitive Science, Rutgers University, New Brunswick, NJ, April 1993. Rutgers Optimality Archive 537 version, 2002.

Alan Prince and Bruce Tesar. 2004. Learning Phonotactic Distributions. In R. Kager, J. Pater, and W. Zonneveld, editors, *Constraints in Phonological Acquisition*, pages 245–291. Cambridge University Press.

Alan Prince. 2002. Entailed Ranking Arguments. ROA 500.

Bruce Tesar. 2008. Output-Driven Maps. ms., Rutgers University; ROA-956.

Roger Webster. 1984. *Convexity*. Oxford University Press.

Learning probabilities over underlying representations

Joe Pater[*]
pater@linguist.umass.edu

Robert Staubs[*]
rstaubs@linguist.umass.edu

Karen Jesney[†]
jesney@usc.edu

Brian Smith[*]
bwsmith@linguist.umass.edu

[*]Department of Linguistics
University of Massachusetts Amherst
Amherst, MA 01003 USA

[†]Department of Linguistics
University of Southern California
Los Angeles, CA 90089 USA

Abstract

We show that a class of cases that has been previously studied in terms of learning of abstract phonological underlying representations (URs) can be handled by a learner that chooses URs from a contextually conditioned distribution over observed surface representations. We implement such a learner in a Maximum Entropy version of Optimality Theory, in which UR learning is an instance of semi-supervised learning. Our objective function incorporates a term aimed to ensure generalization, independently required for phonotactic learning in Optimality Theory, and does not have a bias for single URs for morphemes. This learner is successful on a test language provided by Tesar (2006) as a challenge for UR learning. We also provide successful results on learning of a toy case modeled on French vowel alternations, which have also been previously analyzed in terms of abstract URs. This case includes lexically conditioned variation, an aspect of the data that cannot be handled by abstract URs, showing that in this respect our approach is more general.

1 Introduction

Phonological underlying representations (URs) introduce structural ambiguity. For example, a morpheme that alternates in voicing, like the one meaning 'cat' in Table 1, could have as its underlying representation /bet/ or /bed/, amongst other possibilities. Underlying /bed/ for surface [bet] requires final devoicing, while intervocalic voicing is required for underlying /bet+a/ for [beda] (/-a/ marks the plural). The ambiguity can often be resolved on the basis of further data. For example, if the language includes both voiced and voiceless consonants intervocalically, as in our toy language which also contains [mota], then intervocalic voicing cannot apply across-the-board. The standard phonological analysis, proposed by Jakobson (1948) for similar data from Russian, would thus posit /bed/ as the underlying form for 'cat', as in Table 1, along with a phonological grammar that generates final devoicing.

	UR	SR	Meaning
a.	/bed/	[bet]	cat
b.	/bed+a/	[beda]	cats
c.	/mot/	[mot]	dog
d.	/mot+a/	[mota]	dogs

Table 1: Standard URs for final devoicing

An alternating morpheme can also be given a UR that encodes only the fixed aspects of its structure. For example, 'cat' could have as its UR /beT/, where /T/ represents an alveolar plosive unspecified for voicing. The grammar would then fill in its voicing specification appropriately in both contexts, adding [−voice] finally, and [+voice] intervocalically. One use of this underspecification is to capture instances of three-way contrast. For example, the language in Table 2 has consonants that alternate in voicing, as in the singular and plural of 'cat', as well as consonants that are both fixed voiceless ('dog'/'dogs') and voiced ('pig'/'pigs'). Given the URs shown in Table 2, the surface forms are generated if a grammar fills in voicing on underspecified consonants, and does not change specified ones, as in the analysis of Turkish in Inkelas et al. (1997).

	UR	SR	Meaning
a.	/beT/	[bet]	cat
b.	/beT+a/	[beda]	cats
c.	/mot/	[mot]	dog
d.	/mot+a/	[mota]	dogs
e.	/wid/	[wid]	pig
f.	/wid+a/	[wida]	pigs

Table 2: Underspecified URs and ternary contrast

	UR	SR	Meaning
a.	/bet/	[bet]	cat
b.	/bed+a/	[beda]	cats
c.	/mot/	[mot]	dog
d.	/mot+a/	[mota]	dogs
e.	/wid/	[wid]	pig
f.	/wid+a/	[wida]	pigs

Table 3: UR choice and ternary contrast

There are alternatives to this sort of underspecification. For example, the analysis of Turkish in Becker et al. (2011) posits lexically specific intervocalic voicing, applying to some words but not others. Here we pursue the learning consequences of a proposal in Kager (2008), which involves a grammar that chooses different URs across surface contexts. In this example, /bet/ would be chosen when the morpheme occurs word-finally as in [bet], and /bed/ when it occurs prevocalically, as in [beda] (see Table 3 rows a. and b.). This is a kind of *over*-specification in that the meaning 'cat' has two phonological URs. The non-alternating morphemes /mot/ and /wid/ differ in having only a single UR, with voiceless and voiced final consonants respectively, thus yielding the three-way contrast.

Grammars must be able to choose between URs across surface contexts in order to handle phonologically conditioned suppletive allomorphy - i.e. alternation between forms of a morpheme that are not relatable by a phonological derivation even though the contexts in which each occurs is phonologically defined. The alternation between the forms of the indefinite determiner 'a' and 'an' in English is sometimes analyzed as UR choice, since there is no general process in English of [n] insertion or deletion, but the conditioning context is phonological (vowel- *vs.* consonant-initial following word). That grammars have the power to choose URs in this way is uncontroversial; the only controversies concern the proper formalization of UR choice, and whether particular cases involve UR choice or derivation (Nevins, 2011).

Kager's proposal for ternary contrast is unusual in that it uses UR choice for cases that do seem relatively amenable to analysis in terms of derivations from single URs. Phonologists tend to regard a UR choice analysis as more of a last resort, but as far as we know, there exists no explicit proposal for when an analyst, or a learner, should adopt an analysis with multiple URs for a single morpheme, and when a single UR analysis is required.

One worry about a multiple UR analysis is that it could fail to generalize appropriately. If a learner simply memorized which phonological forms of each morpheme appeared in which contexts, it could fail to extract generalizations, such as the restriction against voicing of word-final consonants in our language in Table 1. This is of course a familiar general issue in learning, and it is the focus of our attention here. We consider a learner to have successfully acquired a language if it finds a grammar that generalizes appropriately, irrespective of the extent to which the learner uses a single phonological UR for each meaning.

Presumably, the assumption that multiple UR analyses of alternations are incompatible with generalization is the basis for their traditional last resort status in phonological theory. However, in at least the grammatical framework that we adopt, and probably in many others, it is possible to construct analyses in which alternations are handled by UR choice, and in which generalizations are still captured. A concrete example is provided by the analysis of the final devoicing language illustrated in Tables 4 and 5, and also by each of the results of the learning simulations presented in sections 3 and 4.

Table 4 shows the distribution over URs that our learner, described with references to precedents in the next section, posits for the final devoicing language. The learner's final grammar is using UR choice to get context-appropriate surface forms of 'cat', as can be seen in rows a. and b. The grammar usually picks /bet/ as the UR for 'cat' when it oc-

	UR	SR	Meaning
a.	/bet/ (0.92) /bed/ (0.08)	[bet]	cat
b.	/bed+a/	[beda]	cats
c.	/mot/	[mot]	dog
d.	/mot+a/	[mota]	dogs

Table 4: Learned URs for final devoicing

Constraint	Devoicing	Contrast
CAT→/bed/	3.65	0
CAT→/bet/	0	0
IDENT-VOICE	6.05	43.62
NO-CODA-VOICE	401.41	39.83
INTER-V-VOICE	1.94	39.83

Table 5: Learned weights

curs finally as in [bet], and almost always picks /bed/ when it occurs prevocalically as in [beda]. This analysis diverges even further from standard phonological practice than Kager's ternary contrast analyses, since we have multiple URs where a single UR analysis would not require underspecification or a lexically specific grammar. Furthermore, in this analysis UR choice is probabilistic, as shown visually in Table 4 row a: /bed/ chosen as the UR in word-final position with probability 0.08. Probabilistic UR choice, which also diverges from the analytic norm in phonology, does not have any observable effect here since the URs neutralize to [bet], but we put it to use in the analysis of French in section 4.

These choices of URs and SRs are being made by a probabilistic weighted constraint version of Optimality Theory (OT) (Prince and Smolensky, 2004), described in the next section. The Input is a string of morphemes ('meanings'), and a candidate is a (UR, SR) pair. Throughout this paper, the candidate URs for a morpheme are all and only its forms observed as SRs (given morphologically segmented words). For the current languages, we include as candidate SRs the identity maps from the URs, and the SRs formed by devoicing any final consonant, or voicing any intervocalic one.

There are three types of constraint. UR constraints (Zuraw, 2000; Boersma, 2001) demand a particular UR for a given morpheme, and are violated when a UR differs from the specified one (Boersma and Zuraw's own formalizations differ somewhat). In Table 5, there are two such constraints, CAT→/bed/ and CAT→/bet/. We omit UR constraints for non-alternating morphemes, since their candidate (UR, SR) pairs always have the same UR, and they always satisfy the single UR constraint. Faithfulness constraints demand (UR, SR) fidelity; here we employ only IDENT-VOICE, which requires a match in voicing specification (McCarthy and Prince, 1999). Finally, Output constraints (AKA Markedness constraints) place demands on the SRs. Here we use NO-CODA-VOICE, which penalizes final voicing, and INTER-V-VOICE, which penalizes an intervocalic voiceless consonant.

Table 5 shows the weights for the constraints that were found for the final devoicing language (Devoicing), and for the language with ternary contrast (Contrast); these yield with high probability the (UR, SR) choices for Tables 4 and 3 respectively. The competition between (/bet/, [bet]) and (/bed/, [bet]) as (UR, SR) pairs for 'cat' illustrates the effects of the first three constraints. The two UR constraints obviously differ in their assessments of the two candidates, as does IDENT-VOICE, which prefers the faithful mapping (/bet/, [bet]) over a voicing change in (/bed/, [bet]). For the final devoicing language, the summed weight of IDENT-VOICE and CAT→/bet/ (6.05) is greater than the weight of CAT→/bed/ (3.65), and so the grammar assigns higher probability to (/bet/, [bet]), as shown in Table 4. For the ternary contrast language on the other hand, the UR constraints have zero weight, and so the decision is fully determined by the relatively high weighted IDENT-VOICE, favoring (/bet/, [bet]).

Even though the learner of the final devoicing language has not acquired the single UR of the traditional phonological analysis, it has acquired a contextually conditioned distribution over UR choices that is appropriate for the learning data. There are weights on the UR constraints that would fail to yield this result. For example, if CAT→/bet/ had a sufficiently high weight relative to the other constraints, then the UR would be fixed as /bet/, and there would be no weighting of the remaining constraints that would pick both [beda] as the highest probability candidate for 'cats', and [mota] as the highest probability candidate for 'dogs'.

Anticipating the discussion of learning in the next section, the weight configuration just described can form a local minimum for our learner. In our simulations, it does not fall into this minimum, nor others like it, when weights are initialized at zero.

The effects of the Output constraints are seen in the choice of URs for 'cat' across phonological contexts in both the final devoicing and ternary contrast languages. NO-CODA-VOICE prefers word-final (/bet/, [bet]) over (/bed/, [bed]), and INTER-V-VOICE prefers intervocalic (/bed+a/, [beda]) over (/bet+a/, [beta]). The high weight on IDENT-VOICE in the ternary contrast language results in very low probability for the unfaithful (UR, SR) mappings (/bed/, [bet]) and (/bet+a/, [beda]). The weights for the coda devoicing language are such that a non-negligible proportion of the probability is reserved for unfaithful (/bed/, [bet]).

Since we have in the case of final devoicing an example of a multiple UR analysis for a language with a phonological regularity, we need to ask whether the grammar generalizes appropriately. The answer is yes. Because of the high weight of NO-CODA-VOICE (401.41) and relatively low weight of IDENT-VOICE (6.05), an underlying voiced obstruent will with extremely high probability map to a surface voiceless one in word-final position. In generating final devoicing this grammar produces predictable relationships between morphologically related words. For example, if a learner with this grammar were to see a plural like [maga] and no singular form, it would posit only /mag/ as the UR for the root. Nonetheless, it would predict with probability near 1 that the singular is pronounced [mak].

Given the observed data from the language in Table 4, it would not have been necessary for the learner to construct a grammar that generalizes in this way. For example, the grammar learned for the ternary contrast language also generates the alternation between [bet] and [bed+a], without producing generalized final devoicing. We thus require a learner with a bias for generalization. Our learner, described in the next section, meets this requirement by incorporating an independently motivated preference for high weighted Output constraints, and low weighted Faithfulness. After describing the learner, we go on to provide simulations for somewhat more complex learning problems.

2 The grammar and learning models

In Maximum Entropy or MaxEnt grammar (Goldwater and Johnson, 2003), the probability of an input/output pair (x_i, y_{ij}) is determined by its *harmony*. The harmony H_{ij} of such a pair is the sum of constraint violations $f_c(x_i, y_{ij})$ scaled by the weights of the constraints w_c.

$$H_{ij} = \sum_c w_c f_c(x_i, y_{ij})$$

This definition of harmony is a common property of grammars that use weighted constraints, as in Harmonic Grammar (Smolensky and Legendre, 2006). A MaxEnt grammar maps harmonies to probabilities, where the probability of a particular output for a particular input $p(y_{ij} \mid x_i)$ is proportional to the exponential of its harmony. These exponentials are normalized within an input, yielding probability distributions.

$$p(y_{ij} \mid x_i) = \frac{1}{Z_i} e^{H_{ij}}$$
$$Z_i = \sum_{j'} e^{H_{ij'}}$$

As discussed above, our output candidates are more elaborate than simple surface forms. Instead, inputs are strings of morphemes and candidates are (UR, SR) pairs. A string of input morphemes x_i can map to an SR y_{ij} in potentially many ways—through many possible URs. Each of these (Input, UR, SR) triples potentially incurs distinct constraint violations. The Input/UR pairing is controlled by the UR constraints, while the UR/SR pairing is controlled by Faithfulness. We thus expand our definition of the probability of a mapping from Input to SR to include all options for the URs z_{ijk}.

$$p(y_{ij} \mid x_i) = \sum_k p(y_{ij}, z_{ijk} \mid x_i)$$

The probabilities $p(y_{ij}, z_{ijk} \mid x_i)$ are defined just as for simple input/output probabilities—they simply include a contribution from candidates on URs. This definition encodes an idea that all URs are potentially valid ways of reaching a particular SR, determined only by the relevant violations of constraints, and does not require a single UR to exist for every Input/SR pairing.

The URs z_{ijk} considered for an input x_i are determined by the UR constraints. A UR z_{ijk} is included in the probability calculation for input x_i only if there exists some constraint $x_i \rightarrow z_{ijk}$. These UR constraints, in turn, rely on observed mappings. For every SR y_{ij} corresponding to an input x_i, we include a UR constraint $x_i \rightarrow y_{ij}$. Thus the candidate URs are simply observed surface forms. In the case of a non-alternating form, only one UR constraint will be included and thus only one UR is entertained. In such cases these constraints are always satisfied; we therefore omit them from our analyses without loss of correctness.

This grammatical framework allows a way of viewing the problem of learning as somewhat agnostic with respect to URs. The learner observes some particular distribution over SRs for a particular input morpheme string and can make any consistent choice about the distribution over URs. It is in this respect that our approach diverges most importantly from prior work on learning URs in Optimality Theory-like frameworks. Our model incorporates ideas from Apoussidou (2007), who uses UR constraints for on-line learning of URs in a probabilistic OT framework, and Eisenstat (2009), who uses a log-linear model very similar to ours. Our approach differs, however, in that learning of unique URs is not taken as a goal.

With the above explicit statement of probabilities, the learner's problem is then to minimize the distinction between its predicted Input/SR distribution and the observed probabilities. For the results presented here, we minimize the Kullback-Leibler (KL) divergence (Kullback and Leibler, 1951) between the predicted distribution p_w and observed distribution p^*.

$$D(p^* \mid\mid p_w) = \sum_i \sum_j p^*(y_{ij} \mid x_i) \log \frac{p^*(y_{ij} \mid x_i)}{p_w(y_{ij} \mid x_i)}$$

We use an L2 (Gaussian) prior (Tychonoff and Arsenin, 1977) on the weights. Such a prior introduces a pressure for lower weights, which is especially important for categorical learning cases (in which KL minimization reduces to likelihood maximization). These problems contain probabilities at unity, causing weights to scale arbitrarily high without additional restriction. We used a regularization with $\sigma^2 = 10,000$ for all solutions presented in this paper.

$$w^* = \underset{w}{\operatorname{argmin}} D(p^* \mid\mid p_w) + \frac{1}{2\sigma^2} \sum_c w_c^2$$

We also include in our prior a term that maximizes the sum of the weights of Output constraints, and minimizes the sum of the weights of Faithfulness constraints. The objective function remains bounded from above by the L2 prior, and is also bounded from below by a restriction to non-negative weights. This term is adapted from research on phonotactic learning in OT starting with Smolensky (1996); see further references in Jesney and Tessier (2011). It resembles somewhat the R-measure of Prince and Tesar (2004), but unlike the R-measure this added prior is continuous, improving performance in optimization.

$$\lambda \left(\sum_{f \in F} w_f - \sum_{o \in O} w_o \right)$$

In experimentation, we found that this term was necessary to ensure generalization; the L2 prior alone, even with a smaller variance for Faithfulness than Output constraints, was insufficient. It might be possible to create a more refined version of this term that is sensitive to dependencies between constraints, but this version has sufficed for our purposes. The scaling factor λ controls the relative importance of generalization compared to KL minimization. For the solutions presented here, the value of λ was chosen on the basis of repeated optimizations. λ was decreased gradually until a criterion level of performance was reached. For categorical cases, this criterion level was a likelihood of greater than 0.95. For non-categorical cases, criterion was a sum squared error of less than 0.05. The minimization problem presented here was solved using the L-BFGS-B method (Byrd et al., 1995) as implemented in R (R Development Core Team, 2010), and all optimizations were constrained to use non-negative weights, with weights initialized at zero.[1]

[1]Scripts and input files are available at http://blogs.umass.edu/hgr/examples-and-other-resources-for-perceptron-and-solver-r/.

	/re-/	/ra:-/	/ró-/	/rú:-/
/-se/	[rése]	[rá:se]	[róse]	[rú:se]
/-sá/	[resá]	[rasá]	[rósa]	[rú:sa]
/-só:/	[resó:]	[rasó:]	[róso]	[rú:so]

Table 6: Abstract UR analysis of Tesar's language

3 Stress-length interaction

To illustrate some of the challenges of UR learning, Tesar (2006) provides the toy language in Table 6. The table shows the phonological results of combining four initial, perhaps root, morphemes with three final, perhaps suffix, morphemes. The phonologically relevant differences between the vowels are in length, marked with a colon, and stress, marked with an acute accent. The rows and columns are labeled with the URs that Tesar posits; we will discuss their justification shortly.

Stressed vowels can either be short or long, but there is an absolute surface restriction against stressless long vowels. The stress-alternating morphemes that have long allomorphs, 'ra' and 'so', show a predictable alternation in length: long when stressed, short when stressless. There is also a preference for stress on roots. Although the suffixes 'sa' and 'so' attract stress over roots 're' and 'ra', they lose their stress to fixed stress roots 'ru' and 'ro', and there are no fixed stress suffixes.

Tesar's URs represent the contrastive properties of the morphemes. The contrast between vowels that are long when stressed and those that are always short is encoded as an underlying difference in length. The contrast between the suffixes that attract stress and those that don't is similarly encoded as an underlying difference in stress, as is the contrast between roots that alternate in stress and those that don't. The abstract UR is /ra:/, which never surfaces in that shape due to the restriction against unstressed long vowels. The vowel must be long to contrast with /re/, and stressless to contrast with /rú:/.

We adopt Tesar's Output and Faithfulness constraints. STRESS-ROOT demands stress on the root, and STRESS-SUFFIX demands stress on the suffix. Output words are limited to a single stress, so one of these constraints is always violated. NO-LONG-UNSTRESS is violated by a surface long stressless vowel. NO-LONG penalizes all long vowels. The Faithfulness constraint IDENT-STRESS demands a (UR, SR) match in stress, and IDENT-LONG demands (UR, SR) fidelity in length. We include in addition a set of UR constraints that demand forms corresponding to each of the observed SRs, except for those that have only a single SR, whose UR is fixed. Candidate SRs for each UR were all combinations of stress on either the root or suffix (not both), and faithful and shortened long vowels.

UR	SR	p	UR	SR	p
/ré+se/	[rése]	0.98	/re+sá/	[resá]	1
/re+se/		0.02			
/re+só:/	[resó:]	1	/rá:+se/	[rá:se]	0.99
			/ra+se/	[ráse]	0.01
/ra+sá/	[rasá]	1	/ra+só:/	[rasó:]	0.99
			/rá:+so/	[rá:so]	0.01
/ró+se/	[róse]	1	/ró+sa/	[rósa]	0.93
			/ró+sá/		0.07
			/ró+sá/	[rosá]	0.01
/ró+so/	[róso]	0.99	/rú:+se/	[rú:se]	1
/ró+só:/	[rosó:]	0.01			
/rú:+sa/	[rú:sa]	0.93	/rú:+so/	[rú:so]	1
/rú:+sá/		0.07			

Table 7: Learned analysis of Tesar's language

The resulting analysis is shown in Table 7, with probabilities rounded to two decimal points. Candidates whose probabilities round to zero are omitted. In all cases a candidate (UR, SR) pair with the correct SR is given highest probability, and is listed in the first row of each cell. Subsequent rows that contain only a UR have the same SR; identical SRs are omitted to aid readability. Given a probabilistic model like a MaxEnt grammar, one cannot define success on a categorical language like this one in terms of granting $p = 1$ to the correct forms, since this will by definition never happen (unless there is only one candidate in a candidate set). Our objective function is stated in terms of maximizing the summed probability of all (UR, SR) pairs that have the correct SR, and an appropriate criterion is therefore to require that the summed probability over full structures be greater for the correct SR than for any other SR. We thus term this simulation successful. We further note that given a MaxEnt grammar that meets this criterion, one can make the probabilities

Constraint	Weight
NO-LONG-UNSTRESS	26.43
STRESS-ROOT	26.05
STRESS-SUFFIX	23.50
IDENT-STRESS	7.66
IDENT-LONG	6.50
'SA'→/sá/	5.04
'SO'→/só:/	4.96
'RE'→/re/	3.85
'RA'→/ra/	3.15
'RA'→/rá:/	0.25
'SO'→/so/	0.02
'SA'→/sa/	0
'RE'→/ré/	0
NO-LONG	0

Table 8: Learned weights for Tesar's language

of the correct forms arbitrarily close to 1 by scaling the weights (multiplying them by some constant).

The constraint weights for the analysis are shown in Table 8. Both of the faithfulness constraints IDENT-STRESS and IDENT-LONG have reasonably high weights, which is expected given the observed contrasts in stress and vowel length across morphemes. The highest probability (UR, SR) mappings are in fact always faithful, with alternations arising from different URs being chosen across phonological contexts.

The crucial case for comparison with the abstract UR analysis is the choice between long stressed /rá:/ and short stressless /ra/, shown with underlining in Table 7. When the morpheme 'ra' combines with 'se', (/rá:+se/, [rá:se]) is preferred to (/ra+se/, [rasé]), partly because it avoids an IDENT-STRESS violation on the suffix, and also partly because of the greater weight of STRESS-ROOT than STRESS-SUFFIX. On the other hand, when the input is 'ra' and 'sa', IDENT-STRESS is no longer at issue since 'sa', unlike 'se', provides the option of a stressed UR. In this case, the sum of the weights of the constraints preferring short stressless /ra/ in (/ra+sá/, [rasá]) is greater than for those preferring /rá:/ in (/rá:+sa/, [rá:sa]). The fixed stress roots differ from 'ra' in not providing the option of a stressless UR, so that a violation of IDENT-STRESS would be incurred if the suffix were stressed. While the constraint interactions are more complex here, UR choice succeeds in replacing underspecification in a parallel fashion to the simpler case of the ternary voicing contrast discussed in the introduction.

The Output constraints sensitive to vowel length are in the expected configuration given the restriction of long vowels to stressed syllables: unviolated NO-LONG-UNSTRESS has a relatively high weight (the highest), while the often-violated NO-LONG, which penalizes all long vowels, has a relatively low weight (the lowest). IDENT-LONG is sandwiched in between, with the result that an underlying long vowel that surfaces in a stressed syllable will retain its length, while one that surfaces in a stressless syllable will be realized as short, with probabilities approaching 1.

Because of the availability of UR choice, the mapping from an underlying long vowel to a surface short stressless one that high-weighted NO-LONG-UNSTRESS generates is never observed in Table 7. However, it is the high probability of this mapping given underlying length and surface stresslessness that ensures that the grammar generalizes appropriately. One paradigmatic regularity in this language is that stressless vowels are short, even when they occur in morphemes whose stressed variants have long vowels. To see how this is captured, imagine that a learner with the grammar in Table 8 were presented with a new morpheme 'su' in combination with 're', which resulted in SR [resú:]. Given the segmentation [re+sú:], it would then form the UR /sú:/, containing the long stressed vowel of the only alternant that it had seen. The morpheme 'ru' also has a single UR, /rú:/, since it is only observed in the learning data as [rú:]. When these are combined as /rú:+sú:/ the resulting SR will be [rú:su], with probability near 1. That is, the grammar generalizes the length alternations, as well as the stress alternations that occur because of the preference for root over suffix stress.

4 Lexically conditioned variation

Here we apply our model to a case of variation, French vowel deletion, which is formalized in terms of candidate SRs having probabilities intermediate between 1 and 0. This case is of particular interest because the probability of deletion varies across

	Word	UR	SR	*p*
a.	femelle	/fømɛl/	[fømɛl]	1
b.	semestre	/sVmɛstʁ/	[sømɛstʁ]	0.8
			[smɛstʁ]	0.2
c.	semelle	/sVmɛl/	[sømɛl]	0.5
			[smɛl]	0.5
d.	Fnac	/fnak/	[fnak]	1
e.	breton	/bʁøtɔ̃/	[bʁøtɔ̃]	1

Table 9: Underspecified URs for French and data

UR V	SR	*p*	UR V	SR	*p*
Y	s'mestre	0.08	Y	s'melle	0.04
N	s'mestre	0.15	N	s'melle	0.45
Y	semestre	0.77	Y	semelle	0.47
N	semestre	0.01	N	semelle	0.03
Y	f'melle	0.09	N	F[ø]nac	0.07
Y	femelle	0.91	N	Fnac	0.93
Y	breton	1			

Table 10: Learned analysis of French

Constraint	Weight
*CCC	467.26
MAX	4.93
'SEMESTRE'→/sømɛstʁ/	4.23
'SEMELLE'→/sømɛl/	2.71
*[ø]	2.58
'SEMELLE'→/smɛl/	0.10
'SEMESTRE'→/smɛstʁ/	0.03
DEP	0.00

Table 11: Learned weights for French

words, which can be captured in terms of differences in weights of UR constraints.

In French, the mid-vowel [ø] is variably deleted (this vowel is sometimes called 'schwa', though it is not an IPA schwa in most varieties). Like one of the toy voicing languages in section 1, French has a ternary contrast, this time in vowel specification. Words either have a non-alternating [ø] ('femelle'), an alternating [ø] ('semestre', 'semelle'), or no [ø] ('Fnac'). The ternary contrast has been analyzed by Anderson (1982) as the result of underspecification.[2] As shown in Table 9, a UR with an underspecified vowel (/V/) is able to be deleted, while a UR with a fully specified vowel (/ø/) is not.

The proportions in Table 9 are partially arbitrary, but accurately reflect the relative probabilities in descriptions such as Dell (1973) and in speaker judgments (Racine, 2007). These show that alternating vowels exhibit a range of deletability. Dictionaries also find the two-way distinction between deleting and non-deleting vowels descriptively inadequate, and a number of experimental and corpus studies find a range of deletion rates across words. Near-minimal pairs in which deletion can occur in both words but at different rates, such as 'semaine' and 'semestre', show that differences in deletion rates cannot be attributed solely to phonological differences, and must be encoded in the the lexicon.

Although [ø]s can be optionally deleted when preceded by a single consonant as in Table 9, [ø] can never be deleted when its deletion would create a three-consonant sequence within a word, as in 'breton' [bʁøtɔ̃]. There are also no words with this sort of three-consonant sequence. In addition to learning the differences in the deletion rates of optional [ø]s, the learner must learn the generalization that an [ø] must be present in the 'breton' environment. Given a /CCC/ input, we want the grammar to avoid the three-consonant cluster by inserting a vowel.

The phonological conditioning of deletion in real French is far more complex than our simple sketch, but this simplified version is sufficient for present purposes. We use the following constraints. The Output constraints *[ø] and *CCC militate against [ø] and three-consonant sequences in the SR, respectively. The faithfulness constraint MAX requires segments in the UR to be present in the SR ('no deletion'), while DEP requires SR segments to be in the UR ('no insertion'). As in the previous sections, UR constraints are only included for morphemes with more than one SR. The learning data consisted of the SRs and probabilities from Table 9.

The resulting analysis is shown in Table 10, using the orthographic convention of marking the lack of a vowel with an apostrophe. The presence of

[2]Anderson (1982) argues that underspecification explains the fact that the alternating vowels can both participate in deletion and alternate with [ɛ], while the non-alternating /ø/ can do neither. However, Morin (1988) presents a number of examples of words that participate in [ɛ]-alternation without participating in deletion.

an underlying vowel is indicated with a 'Y' in the UR column, and its lack with an 'N'. The analysis captures the difference between the rates of [ø] in 'semelle' and 'semestre' as a difference in UR selection. The UR with [ø] is more likely for 'semestre' than 'semelle'. The source of this difference can be seen in the constraint weights in Table 11. The difference between the weights of the UR constraint for 'semestre' requiring the vowel and the one that omits it is greater than that for 'semelle'. The phonological generalization that three-consonant sequences are forbidden is captured by the high weight of *CCC relative to DEP, which means that the grammar will add a vowel to a /CCC/ input.

The contrast between the rates of deletion in 'semelle' and 'semestre' illustrates a widespread phenomenon that is unaddressed by most OT approaches to variation and learning, termed lexically conditioned variation (Coetzee and Pater, 2011). That it is handled in at least this toy version of French is a great benefit of this approach. Underspecification, on the other hand, offers no leverage on this problem, since it provides only a distinction between deleting and non-deleting vowels, and not the finer grained distinctions that the data require.

5 Conclusions

It is a generally unresolved issue how a learner decides whether to use one, or more, URs in an analysis of an alternation. Presumably, learners begin by encoding the various phonological realizations of a morpheme. How, and when, do they decide to collapse these into a single UR? The problem is made more difficult because as noted in the introduction, learners need to consider contextually conditioned UR choice, which is required for at least phonologically conditioned suppletive allomorphy. Previous work on UR learning, including Tesar (2006), abstracts from this issue by allowing only single URs. As a reviewer suggests, a Minimum Description Length criterion might create a bias for fewer URs, but this seems not yet to have been implemented.

In the present approach, phonological generalizations can be acquired even when multiple URs are used, as shown in all of our simulations. This means that the issue raised in the last paragraph can be completely sidestepped by never requiring learners to adopt single URs for alternating morphemes. This approach also sidesteps the difficult issues of choosing which parts of each alternant make up the single UR, and when to leave some structure underspecified. With the French simulation, we have further shown that UR choice handles data that escape underspecification. These advantages suggest that the single UR doctrine, in place since Jakobson (1948), is worth reconsidering, especially in frameworks like OT that can formalize contextual choice of URs without loss of generalization.

One direction for further research is in modeling not only choice between allomorphs, but also their discovery in morpheme segmentation, which involves increasing the size of the hypothesized UR constraint set. Our initial explorations show promise, and this could lead to useful applications in natural language processing, in which MaxEnt models are of course already common. Another extension is to other cases of semi-supervised learning. Here we sum over all of the (UR, SR) pairs corresponding to an observed form. Similar summations can be made over other full structures when the learning data are incomplete: over representations such as syllable structures and syntactic trees, and even over derivations. One such extension that we have explored is to learning 'opacity' (Kiparsky, 1973); see Staubs and Pater (2012) for initial results, which do rely on a type of abstract UR. Finally, one might attempt to model learning of paradigmatic generalizations that are probabilistic across the lexicon, as in Turkish voicing (Becker et al., 2011) - see the related MaxEnt results in Hayes et al. (2009) and Moore-Cantwell (2012).

Acknowledgments

We especially thank Diana Apoussidou and David Smith for their collaboration on earlier presentations of this work, and Mark Johnson for extended discussion. Thanks also to Adam Albright, Paul Boersma, Naomi Feldman, Jeff Heinz, John McCarthy, Paul Smolensky, Colin Wilson and three anonymous reviewers for helpful comments. This research was supported by NSF Grant 0813829 to the University of Massachusetts Amherst, by an NSF Graduate Research Fellowship to Robert Staubs, and a SSHRCC doctoral fellowship to Karen Jesney.

References

Stephen Anderson. 1982. The analysis of french shwa: or how to get something for nothing. *Language*, 58:534–573.

Diana Apoussidou. 2007. *The learnability of metrical phonology*. Ph.D. thesis, University of Amsterdam.

Michael Becker, Nihan Ketrez, and Andrew Nevins. 2011. The surfeit of the stimulus: Analytic biases filter lexical statistics in turkish laryngeal alternations. *Language*, 87:84–125.

Paul Boersma. 2001. Phonology-semantics interaction in OT, and its acquisition. In Robert Kirchner, Wolf Wikeley, and Joe Pater, editors, *Papers in Experimental and Theoretical Linguistics*, volume 6, pages 24–35. University of Alberta, Edmonton.

Richard Byrd, Peihuang Lu, Jorge Nocedal, and Ciyou Zhu. 1995. A limited memory algorithm for bound constrained optimization. *SIAM J. Scientific Computing*, 16:1190–1208.

Andries Coetzee and Joe Pater. 2011. The place of variation in phonological theory. In John Goldsmith, Jason Riggle, and Alan Yu, editors, *The Handbook of Phonological Theory*, pages 401–431. Blackwell, 2nd edition.

François Dell. 1973. *Les règles et les sons. Introduction à la phonologie générative*. Hermann, Paris, 2nd edition.

Sarah Eisenstat. 2009. Learning underlying forms with MaxEnt. Master's thesis, Brown University.

Sharon Goldwater and Mark Johnson. 2003. Learning OT constraint rankings using a maximum entropy model. In *Proceedings of the Stockholm Workshop on Variation within Optimality Theory*, pages 111–120.

Bruce Hayes, Kie Zuraw, Peter Siptar, and Zsuzsa Londe. 2009. Natural and unnatural constraints in Hungarian vowel harmony. *Language*, 85:822–863.

Sharon Inkelas, Cemil Orhan Orgun, and Cheryl Zoll. 1997. The implications of lexical exceptions for the nature of grammar. In *Derivations and Constraints in Phonology*, pages 393–418. Oxford, Clarendon.

Roman Jakobson. 1948. Russian conjugation. *Word*, 4:155–167.

Karen Jesney and Anne-Michelle Tessier. 2011. Biases in Harmonic Grammar: the road to restrictive learning. *Natural Language and Linguistic Theory*, 29:251–290.

René Kager. 2008. Lexical irregularity and the typology of contrast. In Kristin Hanson and Sharon Inkelas, editors, *The Nature of the Word: Studies in Honor of Paul Kiparsky*, pages 397–432. MIT Press.

Paul Kiparsky. 1973. Abstractness, opacity, and global rules. In Osamu Fujimura, editor, *Three Dimensions of Linguistic Theory*, pages 57–86. TEC, Tokyo.

Solomon Kullback and Richard Leibler. 1951. On information and sufficiency. *Annals of Mathematics and Statistics*, pages 22–79.

John McCarthy and Alan Prince. 1999. Faithfulness and identity in prosodic morphology. In René Kager, Harry van der Hulst, and Wim Zonneveld, editors, *The Prosody-Morphology Interface*, pages 218–309. Cambridge University Press.

Claire Moore-Cantwell. 2012. Over- and undergeneralization in derivational morphology. In *NELS Proceedings*.

Yves-Charles Morin. 1988. De l'ajustement du schwa en syllabe fermée dans la phonologie du français. In Hans Basbøll, Yves-Charles Morin, Roland Noske, and Bernard Tranel, editors, *La phonologie du schwa français*, pages 133–189. John Benjamins, Amsterdam.

Andrew Nevins. 2011. Phonologically conditioned allomorph selection. In Colin Ewen, Beth Hume, Marc van Oostendorp, and Keren Rice, editors, *The Companion to Phonology*, pages 2357–2382. Wiley-Blackwell.

Alan Prince and Paul Smolensky. 2004. *Optimality Theory: Constraint interaction in generative grammar*. Blackwell.

Alan Prince and Bruce Tesar. 2004. Learning phonotactic distributions. In René Kager, Joe Pater, and Wim Zonneveld, editors, *Fixing Priorities: Constraints in Phonological Acquisition*, pages 245–291. Cambridge University Press.

R Development Core Team. 2010. R: A language and environment for statistical computing. Technical report, R Foundation for Statistical Computing, Vienna, Austria.

Isabelle Racine. 2007. Effacement du schwa dans des mots lexicaux: constitution d'une base de données et analyse comparative. In *Proceedings of JEL'2007*, pages 125–130. Université de Nantes.

Paul Smolensky and Géraldine Legendre. 2006. *The Harmonic Mind: From Neural Computation to Optimality-Theoretic Grammar*. MIT Press.

Paul Smolensky. 1996. The initial state and 'Richness of the Base' in Optimality Theory. Technical Report JHU-CogSci-96-4, Johns Hopkins University.

Robert Staubs and Joe Pater. 2012. Learning serial constraint-based grammars. In John J. McCarthy and Joe Pater, editors, *Harmonic Grammar and Harmonic Serialism*. Equinox Press.

Bruce Tesar. 2006. Faithful contrastive features in learning. *Cognitive Science*, 30:863–903.

Andrey Nikolayevich Tychonoff and V. Y. Arsenin. 1977. *Solutions of ill-posed problems*. Winston, New York.

Kie Zuraw. 2000. *Exceptions and regularities in phonology*. Ph.D. thesis, UCLA.

Linguistic categorization and complexity

Katya Pertsova
UNC-Chapel Hill
Linguistics Dept, CB 3155
Chapel Hill, NC 27599, USA
pertsova@unc.edu

Abstract

This paper presents a memoryless categorization learner that predicts differences in category complexity found in several psycholinguistic and psychological experiments. In particular, this learner predicts the order of difficulty of learning simple Boolean categories, including the advantage of conjunctive categories over the disjunctive ones (an advantage that is not typically modeled by the statistical approaches). It also models the effect of labeling (positive and negative labels vs. positive labels of two different kinds) on category complexity. This effect has implications for the differences between learning a single category (e.g., a phonological class of segments) vs. a set of non-overlapping categories (e.g., affixes in a morphological paradigm).

1 Introduction

Learning a linguistic structure typically involves categorization. By "categorization" I mean the task of dividing the data into subsets, as in learning what sounds are "legal" and what are "illegal," what morpheme should be used in a particular morphosyntactic context, what part of speech a given words is, and so on. While there is an extensive literature on categorization models within the fields of psychology and formal learning, relatively few connections have been made between this work and learning of linguistic patterns.

One classical finding from the psychological literature is that the subjective complexity of categories corresponding to Boolean connectives follows the order shown in figure 1 (Bruner et al., 1956; Neisser and Weene, 1962; Gottwald, 1971). In psychological experiments subjective complexity is measured in terms of the rate and accuracy of learning an artificial category defined by some (usually visual) features such as color, size, shape, and so on. This finding appears to be consistent with the complexity of isomorphic phonological and morphological linguistic patterns as suggested by typological studies not discussed here for reasons of space (Mielke, 2004; Cysouw, 2003; Clements, 2003; Moreton and Pertsova, 2012). Morphological patterns isomorphic to those in figure 1 appear in figure 2.

The first goal of this paper is to derive the above complexity ranking from a learning bias. While the difficulty of the XOR category is notorious and it is predicted by many models, the relative difference between AND and OR is not. This is because these two categories are complements of each other (so long as all features are binary), and in this sense have the same structure. A memorizing learner can predict the order AND > OR simply because AND has fewer positive examples, but it will also incorrectly predict XOR > OR and AND > AFF. Many popular statistical classification models do not predict the order AND > OR (such as models based on linear classifiers, decision tree classifiers, naive Bayes classifiers, and so on). This is because the same classifier would be found for both of these categories given that AND and OR differ only with respect to what subset of the stimuli is assigned a positive label. Models proposed by psychologists, such as SUSTAIN (Love et al., 2004), RULEX (Nosofsky et al., 1994b), and Configural Cue (Gluck and

AFF (affirmation)	*AND*	*OR*	*XOR/↔*
[●] ▲ [○] △	[●] ▲ ○ △	● [▲] [○] [△]	● [▲] [○] △
circle	circle AND black	triangle OR white	(black AND triangle) OR (white AND circle)

Figure 1: Boolean categories over two features, *shape* and *color*: AFF > AND > OR > XOR

affirmation			*AND*			*OR*			*XOR/↔*		
	sg	pl		sg	pl		sg	pl		sg	pl
−part m.	-	[-im]	−part	[-s]	-	−*poss*	-	[-s]	acc.	-	[-s]
+part m.	-	[-im]	+part	-	-	+*poss*	[-s]	[-s]	nom.	[-s]	-
Hebrew, verb agreement in pres.			English, verb agreement in pres.			English nouns			Old French, o-stem nouns		

Figure 2: Patterns of syncretism isomorphic to the structure of Boolean connectives

Bower, 1988) also do not predict the order AND > OR fore similar reasons. Feldman (2000) speculates that this order is due to a general advantage of the UP-versions of a category over the DOWN-versions (for a category that divides the set of instances into two uneven sets, the UP-version is the version in which the smaller subset is positively labeled, and the DOWN-version is the version in which the larger subset is positively labeled). However, he offers no explanation for this observation. On the other hand, it is known that the choice of representations can affect learnability. For instance, k-DNF formulas are not PAC-learnable while k-CNF formulas describing the same class of patterns are PAC-learnable (Kearns and Vazirani, 1994). Interestingly, this result also shows that conjunctive representations have an advantage over the disjunctive ones because a very simple strategy for learning conjunctions (Valiant, 1984) can be extended to the problem of learning k-CNFs. The learner proposed here includes in its core a similar intersective strategy which is responsible for deriving the order AND > OR.

The second goal of the paper is to provide a unified account of learning one vs. several categories that partition the feature space (the second problem is the problem of learning paradigms). The most straight-forward way of doing this – treating category labels as another feature with n values for n labels – is not satisfactory for several reasons discussed in section 2. In fact, there is empirical evidence that the same pattern is learned differently depending on whether it is presented as learning a distinction between positive and negative instances of a category or whether it is presented as learning two different (non-overlapping) categories. This evidence will be discussed in section 3.

I should stress that the learner proposed here is not designed to be a model of "performance." It makes a number of simplifying assumptions and does not include parameters that are fitted to match the behavioral data. The main goal of the model is to predict the differences in subjective complexity of categories as a function of their logical structure and the presence/absence of negative examples.

2 Learning one versus many categories

Compare the task of learning a phonological inventory with the task of learning an inventory of morph-meaning pairs (as in learning an inflectional paradigm). The first task can be viewed as dividing the set of sounds into attested and non-attested ("accidental gaps"). At first glance, the second task can be analogously viewed as dividing the set of stimuli defined by morpho-syntactic features plus an n-ry feature (for n distinct morphs) into possible vs. impossible combinations of morphs and meanings. However, treating morphs as feature values leads to the possibility of paradigms in which

Neutral (AND/ORn)

	f1	$\overline{f1}$
f2	A	B
$\overline{f2}$	B	B

Biased

ANDb

	f1	$\overline{f1}$
f2	A	$\neg A$
$\overline{f2}$	$\neg A$	$\neg A$

ORb

	f1	$\overline{f1}$
f2	$\neg A$	A
$\overline{f2}$	A	A

Table 1: Three AND/OR conditions in Gottwald's study

different morphs are used with exactly the same set of features as well as paradigms with "accidental gaps," combinations of morpho-syntactic feature values that are impossible in a language. In fact, however, morphs tend to partition the space of possible instances so that no instance is associated with more than one morph. That is, true free variation is really rare (Kroch, 1994). Secondly, system-wide rather than lexical "accidental gaps" are also rare in morphology (Sims, 1996). Therefore, I construe the classification problem in both cases as learning a set of non-overlapping Boolean formulas corresponding to categories. This set can consist of just one formula, corresponding to learning a single category boundary, or it can consist of multiple formulas that partition the feature space, corresponding to learning non-overlapping categories each associated with a different label.

3 Effects of labeling on category complexity

A study by Gottwald (1971) found interesting differences in the subjective complexity of learning patterns in figure 1 depending on whether the data was presented to subjects as learning a single category (stimuli were labeled A vs. $\neg A$) or whether it was presented as learning two distinct categories (the same stimuli were labeled A vs. B). Following this study, I refer to learning a single category as "biased labeling" (abbreviated b) and learning several categories as "neutral labeling" (abbreviated n). Observe that since the AND/OR category divides the stimuli into unequal sets, it has two different biased versions: one biased towards AND and one biased towards OR (as demonstrated in table 1). The order of category complexity found by Gottwald was

AFFn, AFFb > ANDb > AND/ORn > ORb, XORb > XORn

These results show that for the XOR category the neutral labeling was harder than biased labeling. On the other hand, for the AND/OR category the neutral labeling was of intermediate difficulty, and, interestingly, easier than ORb. This is interesting because it goes against an expectation that learning two categories should be harder than learning one category. Pertsova (2012) partially replicated the above finding with morphological stimuli (where null vs. overt marking was the analog of biased vs. neutral labeling). Certain results from this study will be highlighted later.

4 The learning algorithm

This proposal is intended to explain the complexity differences found in learning categories in the lab and in the real world (as evinced by typological facts). I focus on two factors that affect category complexity, the logical structure of a category and the learning mode. The learning mode refers to biased vs. neutral labeling, or, to put it differently, to the difference between learning a single category and learning a partition of a feature space into several categories. The effect of the learning mode on category complexity is derived from the following two assumptions: (i) the algorithm only responds to negative instances when they contradict the current grammar, and (ii) a collection of instances can only be referred to if it is associated with a positive label. The first assumption is motivated by observations of Bruner et. al (1956) that subjects seemed to rely less on negative evidence than on positive evidence even in cases when such evidence was very informative. The second assumption corresponds to a common sentiment that having a linguistic label for a category aids in learning (Xu, 2002).

4.1 Some definitions

For a finite nonempty set of features F, we define the set of *instances* over these features, $I(F)$, as follows. Let R_f be a set of feature values for a feature f (e.g., $R_{height} = \{high, mid, low\}$). Each instance i is a conjunction of feature values given by the functions $f \rightarrow R_f$ for all features $f \in F$. A category is a set of instances that can be described by some non-contradictory Boolean formula ϕ.[1] Namely, ϕ describes a set of instances X if and only if it is logically equivalent to the disjunction of all instances in X. For instance, in the world with three binary features p, q, w, the formula $p \wedge q$ describes the set of instances $\{\{pqw\}, \{pq\bar{w}\}\}$ (where each instance is represented as a set). We will say that a formula ψ *subsumes* a formula ϕ if and only if the set of instances that ψ describes is a superset of the set of instances that ϕ describes. An empty conjunction $\emptyset$ describes the set of all instances.

The goal of the learner is to learn a set of Boolean formulas describing the distribution of positive labels (in the neutral mode all labels are positive, in the biased mode there is one positive label and one negative label). A formula describing the distribution of a label l is encoded as a set of entries of the form e_{l_i} (an i-th entry for label l). The distribution of l is given by $e_{l_1} \vee \ldots \vee e_{l_n}$, the disjunction of n formulas corresponding to entries for l. Each entry e_{l_i} consists of two components: a maximal conjunction ϕ_{max} and an (optional) list of other formulas EX (for exceptions). A particular entry e with two components, $e[\phi_{max}]$ and $e[EX] = \{\phi_1 \ldots \phi_n\}$, defines the formula $e[\phi_{max}] \wedge \neg(\phi_1 \vee \phi_2 \vee \ldots \vee \phi_n)$. $e[\phi_{max}]$ can intuitively be thought of as a rule of thumb for a particular label and EX as a list of exceptions to that rule. In the neutral mode exceptions are pointers to other entries or, more precisely, formulas encoded by those entries. In the biased mode they are formulas corresponding to instances (i.e., conjunctions of feature values for all features). The algorithm knows which mode it is in because the biased mode contains negative labels while the neutral mode does not. Finally, an instance i is *consistent* with an entry e if and only if the conjunction encoded by i logically implies the formula encoded by e. For example, an instance $\{pqw\}$ is consistent with an entry encoding the formula $\{p\}$.

Note that while this grammar can describe arbitrarily complex patterns/partitions, each entry in the neutral learning mode can only describe what linguistics often refer to as "elsewhere" patterns (more precisely Type II patterns in the sense of Pertsova (2011)). And the $e[\phi_{max}]$ component of each entry by definition can only describe conjunctions. There are additional restrictions on the above grammar: (i) the exceptions cannot have a wider distribution than "the rule of thumb" (i.e., an entry e_l cannot correspond to a formula that does not pick out any instances), (ii) no loops in the statement of exceptions is possible: that is, if an entry A is listed as an exception to the entry B, then B cannot also be an exception for A (a more complicated example of a loop involves a longer chain of entries).

When learning a single category, there is only one entry in the grammar. In this case arbitrarily complex categories are encoded as a complement of some conjunction with respect to a number of other conjunctions (corresponding to instances).

4.2 General description

The general organization of the algorithm is as follows. Initially, each positive label is assumed to correspond to a single grammatical entry, and the ϕ_{max} component of this entry is computed incrementally through an intersective generalization strategy that extracts features invariant across all instances used with the same label. When the grammar overgeneralizes by predicting two different labels for at least one instance, exceptions are introduced. The process of exception listing can also lead to overgeneralizations if exceptions are pointers to other entries in the grammar. When these overgeneralizations are detected the algorithm creates another entry for the same label. This latter process can be viewed as positing homophonous entries when learning form-meaning mappings, or as creating multiple "clusters" for a single category as in the prototype model SUSTAIN (Love et al., 2004), and it corresponds to explicitly positing a disjunctive rule. Note that if exceptions are not formulas for other labels, but individual instances, then exception listing does not lead to overgeneralization and no sub-entries are introduced. Thus, when learning a single category the learner generalizes by using an intersective strategy, and then lists exceptions one-by-one as they are discovered in form of negative evidence.

The problem of learning Boolean formulas is known to be hard (Dalmau, 1999). However, it is plausible that human learners employ an algorithm that is not generally efficient, but can easily handle certain restricted types of formulas under certain

[1]The set of Boolean formulas is obtained by closing the set of feature values under the operations of conjunction, negation, and disjunction.

simple distributions of data. (Subclasses of Boolean formulas are efficiently learnable in various learning frameworks (Kearns et al., 1994).) If the learning algorithm can easily learn certain patterns (providing an explanation for what patterns and distributions count as simple), we do not need to require that it be in general efficient.

4.3 Detailed description

First I describe how the grammar is updated in response to the data. The update routine uses a strategy that in word-learning literature is called cross-situational inference. This strategy incrementally filters out features that change from one instance to the next and keeps only those features that remain invariant across the instances that have the same label. Obviously, this strategy leads to overgeneralizations, but not if the category being learned is an affirmation or conjunction. This is because affirmations and conjunctions are defined by a single set of feature values which are shared by all instances of a category (for proof see Pertsova (2007) p. 122). After the entry for a given label has been updated, the algorithm checks whether this entry subsumes or is subsumed by any other entry. If so, this means that there is at least one instance for which several labels are predicted to occur (there is competition among the entries). The algorithm tries to resolve competition by listing more specific entries as exceptions to the more general ones.[2] However there are cases in which this strategy will either not resolve the competition, or not resolve it correctly. In particular, the intermediate entries that are in competition may be such that neither subsumes the other. Or after updating the entries using the intersective strategy one entry may be subsumed by another based on the instances that have been seen so far, but not if we take the whole set of instances into account. These cases are detected when the predictions of the current grammar go against an observed stimulus (step 11 in the function "Update" below). Finally, exception listing fails if it would lead to a "loop" (see section 4.1). The XOR pattern is an example of a simple pattern that will lead to a loop at some point during learning. In general this happens whenever the distribution of the two labels are intertwined in such a way that neither can be stated as a complement of the invariant features of the other.

The following function is used to add an exception:

AddException(expEntry, ruleEntry):

1. **if** adding $expEntry$ to $ruleEntry[EX]$ leads to a loop **then** FAIL
2. **else** add $expEntry$ to $ruleEntry[EX]$

The routine below is called within the main function (presented later); it is used to update the grammar in response to an observed instance x with the label l_i (the index of the label is decided in the main function).

Update

Input: G (current grammar); x (an observed instance), l_i (a label for this instance)

Output: newG

1: newG $\leftarrow$ G
2: **if** $\exists e_{l_i} \in newG$ **then**
3: $\quad e_{l_i}[\phi_{max}] \leftarrow e_{l_i}[\phi_{max}] \cap x$
4: **else**
5: $\quad$ add the entry e_{l_i} to $newG$ with values $e_{l_i}[\phi_{max}] = x$; $e_{l_i}[EX] = \{\}$.
6: **for all** $e_{l'_j} \in newG$ ($e_{l'_j} \neq e_{l_i}$) **do**
7: $\quad$ **if** $e_{l'_j}$ subsumes e_{l_i} **then**
8: $\quad\quad$ AddException($e_{l_i}, e_{l'_j}$)
9: $\quad$ **else if** e_{l_i} subsumes $e_{l'_j}$ **then**
10: $\quad\quad$ AddException($e_{l'_j}, e_{l_i}$)
11: **if** $\exists e_{l'_j} \in newG$ ($l' \neq l$) such that x is consistent with $e_{l'_j}$ **then**
12: $\quad$ AddException($e_{l_i}, e_{l'_j}$)

Before turning to the main function of the algorithm, it is important to note that because a grammar may contain several different entries for a single label, this creates ambiguity for the learner. Namely, in case a grammar contains more than one entry for some label, say two A labels, the learner has to decide after observing a datum (x, A), which entry to update, e_{A_1} or e_{A_2}. I assume that in such cases the learner selects the entry that is most similar to the

[2] This idea is familiar in linguistics from at least the times of Pāṇini. In Distributed Morphology, it is referred to as the Subset Principle for vocabulary insertion (Halle and Marantz, 1993). Similar principles are assumed in rule-ordering systems and in OT (i.e., more specific rules/constraints are typically ordered before the more general ones).

current instance, where similarity is calculated as the number of features shared between x and $e_{A_i}[\phi_{max}]$ (although other metrics of similarity could be explored).

Finally, I would like to note that the value of an entry $e_l(x)$ can change even if the algorithm has not updated this entry. This is because the value of some other entry that is listed as an exception in $e_l(x)$ may change. This is one of the factors contributing to the difference between the neutral and the biased learning modes: if exceptions themselves are entries for other labels, the process of exception listing becomes generalizing.

Main

Input: an instance-label pair (x, l), previous hypothesis G (initially set to an empty set)

Output: newG (new hypothesis)

1: set E to the list of existing entries for the label l in G
2: $k \leftarrow |E|$
3: **if** $E \neq \{\}$ **then**
4:     set $e_{l_{curr}}$ to $e_{l_i} \in E$ that is most similar to x
5:     $E \leftarrow E - e_{l_{curr}}$
6: **else**
7:     $curr \leftarrow k + 1$
8: **if** l is positive **and** $(\neg\exists e_{l_{curr}} \in G$ **or** x is not consistent with $e_{l_{curr}})$ **then**
9:     **if** $update(G, x, l_{curr})$ fails **then**
10:         goto step 3
11:     **else**
12:         $newG \leftarrow update(G, x, l_{curr})$
13: **else if** l is negative and there is an entry e in G consistent with x (positive label was expected) **then**
14:     add x to $e[EX]$ and minimize $e[EX]$ to get $newG$

Notice that the loop triggered when $update$ fails is guaranteed to terminate because when the list of all entries for a label l is exhausted, a new entry is introduced and this entry is guaranteed not to cause $update$ to fail.

This learner will succeed (in the limit) on most presentations of the data, but it may fail to converge on certain patterns if the crucial piece of evidence needed to resolve competition is seen very early on and then never again (it is likely that a human learner would also not converge in such a case).

This algorithm can be additionally augmented by a procedure similar to the selective attention mechanism incorporated into several psychological models of categorization to capture the fact that certain hard problems become easy if a subject can ignore irrelevant features from the outset (Nosofsky et al., 1994a). One (not very efficient, but easy) way to incorporate selective attention into the above algorithm is as follows. Initially set the number of relevant features k to 1. Generate all subsets of F of length k, select one such subset F_k and apply the above learning algorithm assuming that the feature space is F_k. When processing a particular instance, ignore all of its features except those that are in F_k. If we discover two instances that have the same assignment of features in F_k but that appear with two different labels, this means that the selected set of features is not sufficient (recall that free variation is ruled out). Therefore, when this happens we can start over with a new F_k. If all sets of length k have been exhausted, increase k to $k + 1$ and repeat. As a result of this change, patterns definable by smaller number of features would generally be easier to learn than those definable by larger number of features.

5 Predictions of the model for learning Boolean connectives

We can evaluate predictions of this algorithm with respect to category complexity in terms of the proportion of errors it predicts during learning, and in terms of the computational load, roughly measured as the number of required runs through the main loop of the algorithm. Recall that a single data-point may require several such runs if the update routine fails and a new sub-category has to be created.

Below, I discuss how the predictions of this algorithm compare to the subjective complexity ranking found in Gottwald's experiment. First, consider the relative complexity order in the neutral learning mode: AFF > AND/OR > XOR.

In terms of errors, the AFF pattern is predicted to be learned without errors by the above algorithm (since the intersective strategy does not overgeneralize when learning conjunctive patterns). When learning an AND/OR pattern certain orders of data presentation will lead to an intermediate overgeneralization of the label associated with the disjunctive category to the rest of the instances. This will happen if the OR part of the pattern is processed before the AND part. When learning an XOR pattern, the learner is guaranteed to overgeneralize one of the labels on any presentation of the data. Let's walk through the learning of the XOR pattern, repeated below for convenience.

	f1	$\overline{f1}$
f2	A	B
$\overline{f2}$	B	A

Suppose for simplicity that the space of features includes only f1 and f2, and that the first two examples that the learner observes are $(A, \{f1, f2\})$ and $(A, \{\overline{f1}, \overline{f2}\})$. After intersecting $\{f1, f2\}$ and $\{\overline{f1}, \overline{f2}\}$ the learner will overgeneralize A to the whole paradigm. If the next example is $(B, \{f1, \overline{f2}\})$, the learner will partially correct this overgeneralization by assuming that A occurs everywhere except where B does (i.e., except $\{f1, \overline{f2}\}$). But it will continue to incorrectly predict A in the remaining fourth cell that has not been seen yet. When B is observed in that cell, the learner will attempt to update the entry for B through the intersection but this attempt will fail (because the entry for B will subsume the entry for A, but we can't list A as an exception for B since B is already listed as an exception for A). Therefore, a new sub-entry for B, $\{\overline{f1}, f2\}$, will be introduced and listed as another exception for A. Thus, the final grammar will contain entries corresponding to these formulas: $B : (\overline{f1} \wedge f2) \vee (f1 \wedge \overline{f2})$ and $A : \neg((\overline{f1} \wedge f2) \vee (f1 \wedge \overline{f2}))$.

Overall the error pattern predicted by the learner is consistent with the order AFF > AND/OR > XOR.

I now turn to a different measure of complexity based on the number of computational steps needed to learn a pattern (where a single step is equated to a single run of the main function). Note that the speed of learning a particular pattern depends not only on the learning algorithm but also on the distribution of the data. Here I will consider two possible probability distributions which are often used in categorization experiments. In both distributions the stimuli is organized in blocks. In the first one (which I call "instance balanced") each block contains all possible instances repeated once; in the second distribution ("label balanced") each block contains all possible instances with the minimum number of repetitions to insure equal numbers of each label. The distributions differ only for those patterns that have an unequal number of positive/negative labels (e.g., AND/OR). Let us now look at the minimum and maximum number of runs through the main loop of the algorithm required for convergence for each type of pattern. The minimum is computed by finding the shortest sequence of data that leads to convergence and counting the number of runs on this data. The maximum is computed analogously by finding the longest sequence of data. The table below summarizes min. and max. number of runs for the feature space with 3 binary features (8 possible instances) and for two distributions.

	Min	Max (instance)	Max (label)
AFF	4	7	7
AND/OR	4	8	11
XOR	7	9	9

Table 2: Complexity in the neutral mode

The difference between AFF and AND/OR in the number of runs to convergence is more obvious for the label balanced distribution. On the other hand, the difference between AND/OR and XOR is clearer for the instance balanced distribution. This difference is not expected to be large for the label balanced distribution, which is not consistent with Gottwald's experiment in which the stimuli were label balanced, and neutral XOR was significantly more difficult to learn than any other condition.

We now turn to the biased learning mode. Here, the observed order of difficulty was: AFFb > ANDb > ORb, XORb. In terms of errors, both AFFb and ANDb are predicted to be learned with no errors since both are conjunctive categories. ORb is predicted to involve a temporary overgeneralization of the positive label to the negative contexts. The same is true for XORb except that the proportion of errors will be higher than for ORb (since the latter category has fewer negative instances).

The minimum and maximum number of runs required to converge on the biased categories for two types of distributions (instance balanced and label balanced) is given below. Notice that the minimum numbers are lower than in the previous table because in the biased mode some categories can be learned from positive examples alone.

	Min	Max (instance)	Max (label)
AFFb	2	7	7
ANDb	2	8	8
ORb	4	16	22
XORb	6	16	16

Table 3: Complexity in the biased mode

The difference between affirmation and conjunction is not very large which is not surprising (both are conjunctive categories). Again we see that the two types of distributions give us slightly different predictions. While ANDb seems to be learned faster than ORb in both distributions, it is not clear whether and to what extent ORb and XORb are on average different from each other in the label balanced distribution. Recall that Gottwald found no significant difference between ORb and XORb (in fact numerically ORb was harder than XORb). Interestingly, in a morphological analogue of Gottwald's study in which the number of instances rather than labels was balanced, I found the opposite difference: ORb was easier to learn than XORb (the number of people to reach learning criterion was 8 vs. 4 correspondingly) although the difference in error rates on the testing trials was not significant (Pertsova, 2012). More testing is needed to confirm whether the relative difficulty of these two categories is reliably affected by the type of distribution as predicted by the learner.[3]

Finally, we look at the effect of labeling within each condition. In the AFF condition, Gottwald found no significant difference between neutral labeling and biased labeling. This could be due to the fact that subjects were already almost at ceiling in learning this pattern (median number of trials to convergence for both conditions was ≤ 5). In the AND/OR condition, Gottwald observed the interesting order ANDb > AND/OR > ORb. This order is also predicted by the current algorithm. Namely, the neutral category AND/OR is predicted to be harder than ANDb because (1) ANDb requires less computational resources (2) on some distributions of data overgeneralization will occur when learning an AND/OR pattern but not an ANDb category. The AND/OR > ORb order is also predicted and is particularly pronounced for label balanced distribution. Since two labels are available when learning the AND/OR pattern, the AND portion of the pattern can be learned quickly and subsequently listed as an exception for the OR portion (which becomes the"elsewhere" case). On the other hand, when learning the ORb category, the conjunctive part of the pattern is initially ignored because it is not associated with a label. The learner only starts paying attention to negative instances when it overgeneralizes. For a similar reason, the biased XOR category is predicted to be harder to learn than the neutral XOR category. This latter prediction is not consistent with Gottwald's finding, who found XORn not just harder than other categories but virtually impossible to learn: 6 out of 8 subjects in this condition failed to learn it after more than 256 trials. In contrast to this result (and in line with the predictions of the present learner), Pertsova (2012) found that the neutral XOR condition was learned by 8 out of 12 subjects on less than 64 trials compared to only 4 out of 12 subjects in the biased XOR condition.

To conclude this section, almost all complexity rankings discussed in this paper are predicted by the proposed algorithm. This includes the difficult to model AND > OR ranking which obtains in the biased learning mode. The only exception is the neutral XOR pattern, which was really difficult to learn in Gottwald's non-linguistic experiment (but not in Pertsova's morphological experiment), and which is not predicted to be more difficult than biased XOR. Further empirical testing is needed to clarify the effect of labeling within the XOR condition.

[3] Another possible reason for the fact that Gottwald did not find a difference between ORb and XORb is this: if selective attention is used during learning, it will take longer for the learner to realize that ORb requires the use of two features compared to XORb especially when the number of positive and negative examples are balanced. In particular, a one feature analysis of ORb can explain 5/6 of the data with label balanced stimuli, while a one feature analysis of XORb can only explain 1/2 of the data, so it will be quickly abandoned.

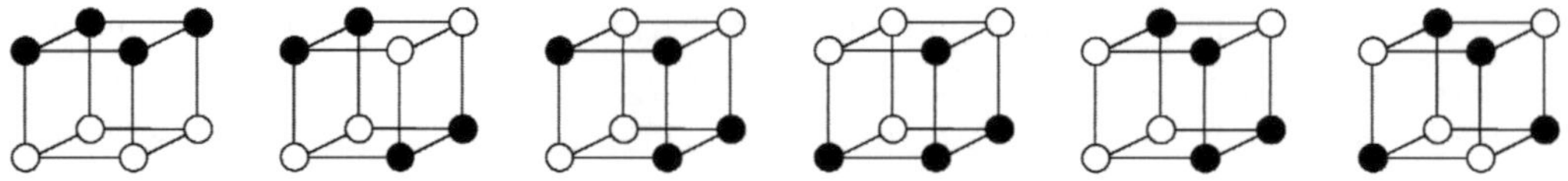

Figure 3: Shepard et. al. hierarchy

6 Other predictions

Another well-studied hierarchy of category complexity is the hierarchy of symmetric patterns (4 positive and 4 negative instances) in the space of three binary features originally established by Shepard et. al (1961). These patterns are shown in figure 3 using cubes to represent the three dimensional feature space.

Most studies find the following order of complexity for the Shepad patterns: I > II > III, IV, V > VI (Shepard et al., 1961; Nosofsky et al., 1994a; Love, 2002; Smith et al., 2004). However, a few studies find different rankings for some of these patterns. In particular, Love (2002) finds IV > II with a switch to unsupervised training procedure. Nosofsky and Palmeri (1996) find the numerical order I > IV > III > V > II > VI with intergral stimulus dimensions (feature values that are difficult to pay selective attention to independent of other features, e.g., hue, brightness, saturation). More recently Moreton and Persova (2012) also found the order IV > III > V, VI (as well as I > II, III, > VI) in an unsupervised phonotactics learning experiment.

So, one might wonder what predictions does the present learner make with respect to these patterns. We already know that it predicts Type I (affirmation) to be easier than all other types. For the rest of the patterns the predictions in terms of speed of acquisition are II > III > IV, V > VI in the neutral learning mode (similar to the typical findings). In the biased learning mode, patterns II through VI are predicted to be learned roughly at the same speed (since all require listing four exceptions). If selective attention is used, Type II will be the second easiest to learn after Type I because it can be stated using only two features. However, based on the error rates, the order of difficulty is predicted to be I > IV > III > V > II > VI (similar to the order found by Nosofsky and Palmeri (1996)). No errors are ever made with Type I. The proportion of errors in other patterns depends on how closely the positive examples cluster to each other. For instance, when learning a Type VI pattern (in the biased mode) the learner's grammar will be correct on 6 out of 8 instances after seeing any two positive examples (the same is not true for any other pattern, although it is almost true for III). After seeing the next instance (depending on what it is and on the previous input) the accuracy of the grammar will either stay the same, go up to 7/8, or go down to 1/2. But the latter event has the lowest probability. Note that this learner predicts non-monotonic behavior: it is possible that a later grammar is less accurate than the previous grammar. So, for a non-monotonic learner the predictions based on the speed of acquisition and accuracy do not necessarily coincide.

There are many differences across the categorization experiments that may be responsible for the different rankings. More work is needed to control for such differences and to pin down the sources for different complexity results found with the patterns in figure 3.

7 Summary

The current proposal presents a unified account for learning a single category and a set of categories partitioning the stimuli space. It is consistent with many predictions about subjective complexity rankings of simple categories, including the ranking AND > OR, not predicted by most categorization models, and the difference between the biased and the neutral learning modes not previously modeled to my knowledge.

References

Jerome S. Bruner, Jacqueline J. Goodnow, and George A. Austin. 1956. *A study of thinking*. John Wiley and Sons, New York.

George N. Clements. 2003. Feature economy in sound systems. *Phonology*, 20(3):287–333.

Michael Cysouw. 2003. *The paradigmatic structure of person marking*. Oxford studies in typology and linguistic theory. Oxford University Press, Oxford.

Víctor Dalmau. 1999. Boolean formulas are hard to learn for most gate bases. In Osamu Watanabe and Takashi Yokomori, editors, *Algorithmic Learning Theory*, volume 1720 of *Lecture Notes in Computer Science*, pages 301–312. Springer Berlin / Heidelberg.

Jacob Feldman. 2000. Minimization of Boolean complexity in human concept learning. *Nature*, 407:630–633.

Mark A. Gluck and Gordon H. Bower. 1988. evaluating an adaptive network model of human learning. *Journal of memory and language*, 27:166–195.

Richard L. Gottwald. 1971. Effects of response labels in concept attainment. *Journal of Experimental Psychology*, 91(1):30–33.

Morris Halle and Alec Marantz. 1993. Distributed morphology and the pieces of inflection. In K. Hale and S. J. Keyser, editors, *The View from Building 20*, pages 111–176. MIT Press, Cambridge, Mass.

Michael Kearns and Umesh Vazirani. 1994. *An introduction to computational learning theory*. MIT Press, Cambridge, MA.

Michael Kearns, Ming Li, and Leslie Valiant. 1994. Learning boolean formulas. *J. ACM*, 41(6):1298–1328, November.

Anthony Kroch. 1994. Morphosyntactic variation. In Katharine Beals et al., editor, *Papers from the 30th regional meeting of the Chicago Linguistics Society: Parasession on variation and linguistic theory*. Chicago Linguistics Society, Chicago.

Bradley C. Love, Douglas L. Medin, and Todd M. Gureckis. 2004. SUSTAIN: a network model of category learning. *Psychological Review*, 111(2):309–332.

Bradley C. Love. 2002. Comparing supervised and unsupervised category learning. *Psychonomic Bulletin and Review*, 9(4):829–835.

Jeff Mielke. 2004. *The emergence of distinctive features*. Ph.D. thesis, Ohio State University.

Elliott Moreton and Katya Pertsova. 2012. Is phonological learning special? Handout from a talk at the 48th Meeting of the Chicago Society of Linguistics, April.

Ulrich Neisser and Paul Weene. 1962. Hierarchies in concept attainment. *Journal of Experimental Psychology*, 64(6):640–645.

Robert M. Nosofsky and Thomas J. Palmeri. 1996. Learning to classify integral-dimension stimuli. *Psychonomic Bulletin and Review*, 3(2):222–226.

Robert M. Nosofsky, Mark A. Gluck, Thomas J. Palmeri, Stephen C. McKinley, and Paul Gauthier. 1994a. Comparing models of rule-based classification learning: a replication and extension of Shepard, Hovland, and Jenkins (1961). *Memory and Cognition*, 22(3):352–369.

Robert M. Nosofsky, Thomas J. Palmeri, and Stephen C. McKinley. 1994b. Rule-plus-exception model of classification learning. *Psychological Review*, 101(1):53–79.

Katya Pertsova. 2007. *Learning Form-Meaning Mappings in the Presence of Homonymy*. Ph.D. thesis, UCLA.

Katya Pertsova. 2011. Grounding systematic syncretism in learning. *Linguistic Inquiry*, 42(2):225–266.

Katya Pertsova. 2012. Logical complexity in morphological learning. In *Proceedings of the 38th Annual Meeting of the Berkeley Linguistics Society*.

Roger N. Shepard, C. L. Hovland, and H. M. Jenkins. 1961. Learning and memorization of classifications. *Psychological Monographs*, 75(13, Whole No. 517).

Andrea Sims. 1996. *Minding the Gaps: inflectional defectiveness in a paradigmatic theory*. Ph.D. thesis, The Ohio State University.

J. David Smith, John Paul Minda, and David A. Washburn. 2004. Category learning in rhesus monkeys: a study of the Shepard, Hovland, and Jenkins (1961) tasks. *Journal of Experimental Psychology: General*, 133(3):398–404.

Leslie G. Valiant. 1984. A theory of the learnable. In *Proceedings of the sixteenth annual ACM symposium on Theory of computing*, STOC '84, pages 436–445, New York, NY, USA. ACM.

Fei Xu. 2002. The role of language in acquiring object kind concepts in infancy. *Cognition*, 85(3):223 – 250.

Author Index